T5-BPY-486

DEATH AND IMMORTALITY

ROY W. PERRETT

University of Otago, Dunedin, New Zealand

1987 **MARTINUS NIJHOFF PUBLISHERS**
a member of the KLUWER ACADEMIC PUBLISHERS GROUP
DORDRECHT / BOSTON / LANCASTER

BD
444
.P469
1987

Distributors

for the United States and Canada: Kluwer Academic Publishers, P.O. Box 358, Accord Station, Hingham, MA 02018-0358, USA
for the UK and Ireland: Kluwer Academic Publishers, MTP Press Limited, Falcon House, Queen Square, Lancaster LA1 1RN, UK
for all other countries: Kluwer Academic Publishers Group, Distribution Center, P.O. Box 322, 3300 AH Dordrecht, The Netherlands

Library of Congress Cataloging in Publication Data

```
Perrett, Roy W.
  Death and immortality.

  (Studies in philosophy and religion ; 10)
  Bibliography: p.
  Includes index.
  1. Death. 2. Immorality. I. Title. II. Series:
Studies in philosophy and religion ; v. 10.
BD444.P469 1986         129         86-23769
IBBN 90-247-3440-1
```

ISBN 90-247-3440-1
ISBN 90-247-2346-9 (series)

Copyright

© 1987 by Martinus Nijhoff Publishers, Dordrecht.

All rights reserved. No part of this publication may be reproduced, stored in a retrieval system, or transmitted in any form or by any means, mechanical, photocopying, recording, or otherwise, without the prior written permission of the publishers,
Martinus Nijhoff Publishers, P.O. Box 163, 3300 AD Dordrecht,
The Netherlands.

PRINTED IN THE NETHERLANDS

DEATH AND IMMORTALITY

STUDIES IN PHILOSOPHY AND RELIGION

1. FREUND, E.R. *Franz Rosenzweig's Philosophy of Existence: An Analysis of* The Star of Redemption. 1979. ISBN 90 247 2091 5.

2. OLSON, A.M. *Transcendence and Hermeneutics: An Interpretation of the Philosophy of Karl Jaspers*. 1979. ISBN 90 247 2092 3.

3. VERDU, A. *The Philosophy of Buddhism*. 1981. ISBN 90 247 2224 1.

4. OLIVER, H.H. *A Relational Metaphysic*. 1981. ISBN 90 247 2457 0.

5. ARAPURA, J.G. *Gnosis and the Question of Thought in Vedānta*. 1986. ISBN 90 247 3061 9.

6. HOROSZ, W. and CLEMENTS, T. *Religion and Human Purpose*. 1986. ISBN 90 247 3000 7.

7. SIA, S. *God in Process Thought*. 1985. ISBN 90 247 3103 8.

8. KOBLER, J.F. *Vatican II and Phenomenology*. 1985. ISBN 90 247 3193 3.

9. GODFREY, J.J. *A Philosophy of Human Hope*. 1986. ISBN 90 247 3353 7.

10. PERRETT, R.W. *Death and Immortality*. 1987. ISBN 90 247 3440 1.

In Memoriam

Jim Harvie

PREFACE

The research for this work was undertaken during my tenure of a Senior Tutorship in the Faculty of Arts and Music at the University of Otago (1983-85). Versions of some of the chapters herein have already been accepted for publication in the form of journal articles in *Philosophy*, *Philosophy East and West*, *Sophia*, and *Religious Studies*. My thanks to the editors and publishers concerned for permission to reuse this material.

A number of people have assisted me in various ways. My greatest debt is to Graham Oddie, who supervised my doctoral research in this area and with whom I have had the benefit of innumerable discussions on these and other philosophical matters. I am very grateful for all I have learned from him. I would also like to thank: Bob Durrant for commenting helpfully on Chapter 2; the late Jim Harvie, both for his valuable suggestions (particularly regarding the material of Chapter 4) and for his encouraging enthusiasm for the whole project; George Hughes for his extensive comments on the whole work; and (for various points of detail) Alan Musgrave, Charles Pigden and Bryan Wilson. Despite much good advice, however, I have sometimes preferred to go my own way, recalling Blake's proverb: "If the fool would persist in his folly he would become wise."

With regard to the typing of the manuscript I am indebted to the word-processor wizardry of Jane Tannahill and Christine Colbert. Most particularly, however, I am grateful to Bryan Wilson for all his efforts in preparing the camera-ready copy of this work.

Finally, my love and special thanks to Val, Sara and Anna for putting up with it all.

CONTENTS

INTRODUCTION

In *The World as Will and Representation* Schopenhauer writes:

Death is the real inspiring genius or Musagetes of philosophy, and for this reason Socrates defined philosophy as θανάτου μελέτη [preparation for death]. Indeed, without death there would hardly have been any philosophizing (II, 463).

For this to be plausible it would have to be added that death is most often the unconscious muse of philosophy; certainly it is difficult to see much contemporary professional philosophy as standing squarely within the Socratic tradition Schopenhauer here alludes to. This work, however, is self-avowedly inspired by death. It discusses a number of philosophical problems of death and immortality: particularly certain questions in metaphysics, ethics and philosophy of religion which naturally arise from philosophical reflection upon these matters. However since philosophical concepts and arguments are embedded in a network of other concepts and arguments, the inquiry sometimes involves both the consideration of issues in other areas of philosophy (including epistemology and metaphilosophy) and in areas other than philosophy (including literature, theology and religious studies).

Concern with death and immortality is, of course, universal and hence the literature is enormous. Obviously I could not discuss everything, even if *per impossibile* I had read it all. The principles governing my choice of material are largely generated by the philosophical style I work in, i.e. the style of the analytic tradition that dominates contemporary Anglo-American philosophy. Thus although the great Western philosophers are often mentioned, their positions receive little historical attention. Similarly, except for a brief reference to Heidegger, I do not discuss recent Continental philosophers at all. Rather I usually prefer to develop positions with particular reference to contemporary discussions in the analytic tradition. This is not because I believe that the great figures of the past have nothing to say to us on these issues; nor do I mean to denigrate recent Continental contributions. However this work is primarily conceived of as an attempt to demonstrate the relevance of the methods of analytic philosophy for traditional philosophical concerns about death and immortality. Until quite recently many analytic philosophers too often regarded such concerns as falling outside of the competence of philosophy. Fortunately there are now signs of an increasing openness to such questions among more and more philosophers within the analytic tradition. This work is an attempt to foster this trend. Of course, there is a danger that the constraints thus imposed upon the inquiry will render the resulting work too parochial. I have deliberately attempted to rectify any such tendency to narrowness by introducing some sorts of relevant material from outside of the usual ambit of analytic philosophy. In particular, I not only discuss literary and theological works, but I also give detailed consideration to concepts and arguments drawn from the Indian philosophical tradition. My aim is to show both that such material has important insights to contribute and also that it is in fact amenable to rigorous examination.

It will perhaps be convenient before we begin the inquiry proper to offer an outline of the overall structure of the argument. Briefly, this work divides into two parts: the first part discusses philosophical problems about death that arise for everyone, regardless of his or her stance on immortality; the second part focuses on the notion of immortality and the major traditional accounts of this. Chapter 1 presents a discussion of the concept of death (including the troubled question of "defining" death) and considers the epistemic status of our knowledge of death. Chapter 2 considers the claim that it is impossible to imagine one's own death and what the significance of this might be if it is indeed true. Chapter 3 argues that (*contra* the Epicurean tradition) the fear of death is rational under certain conditions. Chapter 4 discusses some more general questions about the relation of death to the meaning of life, arguing by way of a consideration of Tolstoy's *A Confession* and *The Death of Ivan Ilych* that immortality is not a necessary condition for the meaningfulness of life.

Chapter 5 argues that immortality is not a sufficient condition for the meaningfulness of life either. Of course, "eternal life" has typically referred to a transformed quality of life in the hereafter according to most religious thinkers. Some writers, however, wish to understand "eternal life" as referring only to a quality of life *now*, with no eschatological implications (e.g. Tolstoy, D. Z. Phillips). This view often goes with a conviction that traditional conceptions of immortality are incoherent. The remaining three chapters of the second part of the work critically address this conviction. Disembodied existence is found to face an identity problem, though it is suggested that the Hindu monistic eschatology of Advaita Vedānta can meet this difficulty at a certain cost. Resurrection is argued to be a metaphysically coherent doctrine, as also is the general Indian account of rebirth.

Finally, the Postscript offers some concluding remarks about the main part of the investigation and the Appendix (on karma and the problem of suffering) discusses a topic that is relevant but somewhat tangential to the thrust of the central argument. There the viability of karma is defended against the charge that it involves a vicious explanatory regress.

PART ONE:

DEATH

CHAPTER 1: DEATH

The obvious place to begin our inquiry is with an examination of the concept of death. As it happens, in recent years there has been considerable discussion in medical and legal circles about the definition of death.[1] Of course, physicians have always been concerned with the matter of a reliable sign of death. However, until recently their chief concern was the prevention of premature burial. Today the question has acquired urgency because of a number of advances in medical science, particularly in the technology of artificial life-support systems and in the techniques of organ transplantation. These life-support systems can artificially sustain functions like heart beat, the absence of which was formerly taken to be evidence of death. A patient's heart can still be beating with the aid of a respirator though a flat EEG reading indicates "brain-death". Should the respirator be turned off, given that the "brain-dead" patient is making economic demands on scarce hospital resources and huge psychological demands on relatives? Moreover, if the patient possesses functioning organs that can be donated for transplantation purposes then the question of the significance and definition of death is further complicated. The sooner the organs are removed from the body after somatic death (i.e. the extinction of personality), the better the chance of the graft taking. Hence deciding when the patient is dead becomes extremely important since the organs must be "alive" to be valuable while, of course, the donor must be "dead" in order that they can be removed. These ethical problems in turn also pose legal difficulties. Thus not only do physicians face litigation from

---

[1] See *inter alia* the following sources and the references cited therein: A. Keith Mant, "The Medical Definition of Death" in Arnold Toynbee *et al., Man's Concern With Death* (London: Hodder and Stoughton, 1968), pp. 13-24; Peter McL. Black, "Three Definitions of Death" *The Monist* **60** (1977): 136-146; Douglas N. Walton, *On Defining Death* (Montreal: McGill-Queen's University Press, 1979), especially Ch. III; Robert F. Weir, ed., *Ethical Issues in Death and Dying* (New York: Columbia University Press, 1977), Part Two; Tom L. Beauchamp and Seymour Perlin, eds., *Ethical Issues in Death and Dying* (Englewood Cliffs, N.J.: Prentice-Hall, 1978), Part 1; P. D. G. Skegg, *Law, Ethics, and Medicine* (Oxford: Clarendon Press, 1984), Ch. 9.

relatives of the patient, but many have hoped for a legal definition of death that would help resolve the bioethical issues.

Now I don't so much wish to adjudicate on what the medical or legal definition of death should be (though I certainly believe that the bioethical issues cannot be "defined away"). However, I do wish to comment upon the evident misunderstandings of the conceptual status of some of the principal candidates that have been offered for the job and of the nature of the problem that is involved in attempting to define death. And this task is clearly a *philosophical*, rather than a medical or legal, one.

In this connection let's consider first the legal definition offered in *Black's Law Dictionary* (rev. 4th edition, 1968) where death is stated to be:

> The cessation of life; the ceasing to exist; defined by physicians as a total stoppage of the circulation of the blood, and a cessation of the animal and vital functions consequent thereon, such as respiration, pulsation, etc.[2]

There is much wrong with this definition. First, to say death is "the cessation of life; the ceasing to exist" is not very helpful in practical legal terms, for it just saddles us with the problem of the meaning of "life". Second, it is now false that physicians define death as "total stoppage of the circulation of the blood etc." There is widespread concern to establish "brain-death" or other criteria as defining death. Third, "total stoppage of the circulation of the blood etc." are clearly not necessary and sufficient conditions of being dead, as seems intended here. A person who has been decapitated or hanged is presumably dead though spontaneous vital functions may continue for several minutes after the act of execution has taken place. Or again, suppose I suffer a heart attack and my heart stops. Fortunately medical assistance is at hand and the doctors manage to return my heart to normal function and revive me. Was I dead for the time my heart had stopped and I was not breathing? Surely not, for if it is indeed

---

[2] This definition has been abandoned in the 5th edition (1979) in favour of: "The cessation of life; permanent cessations of all vital functions and signs. Numerous states have enacted statutory definitions of death which include brain-related criteria." This revised effort avoids some of my criticisms of the earlier version, but at the expense of being even more vacuous as a practical legal definition.

claimed that I was dead then the definition seems to have some odd legal consequences. Thus my wife is presumably entitled to collect on my life insurance so that I can help her spend it, and the person whose blow caused my death will be charged with homicide at a trial I will be able to attend. Cardiac and respiratory inactivity are not sufficient conditions for death. Nor will it do to construe "total stoppage" in such a way that it includes the idea of *irreversible* inactivity. In the first place we then have the epistemic problem of deciding whether the inactivity is ever irreversible. In the second place such a move would make it analytically true that no one could be physically resurrected. But the claim that I shall be resurrected, though possibly false, is not obviously self-contradictory. Finally, whether the proposed conditions are even necessary is precisely what physicians are disputing, for on this definition a comatose patient with massive head injuries could (in principle) remain indefinitely on a respirator, his heart still beating. Could he ever be declared dead?

It is this latter question that is addressed in the much discussed paper "A Definition of Irreversible Coma" written in 1968 by an Ad Hoc Committee of the Harvard Medical School.[3] It proposes that death be defined by means of a new criterion: irreversible coma. This is to be determined when, (given the absence of hypothermia or drug overdose as prior conditions), examination on two occasions 24 hours apart reveals unreceptivity and unresponsivity to all stimuli, no movement or breathing, no reflexes and a flat EEG reading. On this definition the brain-dead patient on the respirator is dead, even if his heart is beating.

But note also the form of this definition. It offers not a set of necessary and sufficient conditions, but rather a set of operational criteria. In this sense it might be argued that it is not a *definition* of death at all. It does not seek to answer the *semantic* question about the concept of death, but rather addresses the *epistemic* question of how to determine whether a patient is indeed dead by providing operational criteria for

---

[3] Reprinted in Weir, pp. 82-89; Beauchamp and Perlin, pp. 11-18. The suggestion that brain-death is a definition of death, or at least a criterion of death, is resisted in Lawrence C. Becker, "Human Being: The Boundaries of the Concept" *Philosophy & Public Affairs* **4** (1975): 334-359 (see especially section IV). The brain-death definition is defended in David Lamb, "Diagnosing Death" *Philosophy & Public Affairs* **7** (1978): 144-153; and in Michael B. Green and Daniel Wikler, "Brain Death and Personal Identity" *Philosophy & Public Affairs* **9** (1980): 105-133.

that purpose. Note too that by explicitly bringing in the notion of irreversibility it opens up further epistemic problems about when *irreversible* coma can justifiably be declared. Is 24 hours just an arbitrary time limit to set up? Finally, by identifying death in this way with brain-death it seems to follow that life is to be identified with "brain-life", i.e. recognizable neurological activity. This seems not only to beg a number of philosophical questions, but also to have important practical ramifications. Would it follow that a foetus is not alive until it has recognizable mental activity? The implications for the morality of abortion are obvious.

All of this does not mean, however, that there is nothing of value in the legal and medical attempts at defining death which we have been looking at. Rather, the real problem with them is that they tend to conflate the question of what death is with the question of how to determine whether death has occurred. Criteria proffered to settle the latter question cannot in themselves settle the former question; indeed the former question is logically prior to the latter one. Of course, this point has not gone completely unnoticed by other writers on the topic. The philosopher Douglas Walton, for example, takes the already mentioned view that the kind of medical criteria proposed by the Harvard Committee and other bodies are operational criteria designed to answer the epistemic question, "When can we know the patient is dead?" He distinguishes the latter question from the philosophical semantic question, "What is death?" He is content to leave the first question to the physicians and the second to the philosophers, with the philosophers' results providing the necessary check on the physicians' activities. Presumably the physicians have to wait on the philosophical work here, for there is limited value in devising tests to measure something the identity of which they are ignorant. What would they be trying to measure?

However Walton then goes on to distinguish two separate conceptions of death: the *secular* and the *religious*. The secular conception of death is "total and irreversible extinction of consciousness and sensation, including discontinuation of actual survival of the individual personality"; whereas the religious conception of death "postulates actual survival of the individual personality and continuation of *post mortem* consciousness and sensation."[4] But which of these two different concepts is instantiated

---

[4] Walton, p. 41.

when an individual dies and how do the operational criteria enable us to know? Surely both conceptions cannot be correct. Or perhaps do some people "die" in the secular sense and some in the religious sense? Nor does it seem that secular and religious people mean something different by "death", though they may indeed have different expectations about the possibility of life after death. Finally, suppose we find out that the secularist is right and no one survives her death. Is the religious person now to retort that the discovery of this truth means that after all no one "dies" and hence we are all presumably "immortal"? It seems, then, that this sort of philosophical approach to the task of defining death is just as problematic as the legal attempt in terms of necessary and sufficient conditions or the medical attempt in terms of operational criteria.

What might be a more promising philosophical approach to understanding the concept of death then? I suggest we begin with a distinction that has become of central importance in connection with the debate on questions like abortion and infanticide: viz. the distinction between *persons* and *human beings*.[5] The concept of a human being (i.e. a living organism of the biological species *Homo sapiens*) is importantly distinct from the concept of a person. One argument for the distinctness of these two concepts is that it is possible for a person to cease to exist without any biological organism having been destroyed — consider science fiction cases where the same body is successively inhabited by different persons. A second argument draws on other sorts of science fiction cases where we have beings that we would want to count as persons, but who belong to a species biologically distinct from us. A third argument (less widely accepted) is that some non-human animals are persons.

Utilizing this distinction Michael Tooley has argued that the term "death" is ambiguous when applied to sentient organisms.[6] We might be referring either (i) to the death of the biological organism or (ii) to the death of the associated person. Tooley then goes on to make two further claims. First, that the morally relevant

---

[5] For an extended discussion of this distinction see Michael Tooley, *Abortion and Infanticide* (Oxford: Clarendon Press, 1983), Ch. 4.

[6] Michael Tooley, "Decisions to Terminate Life and the Concept of Person" in John Ladd, ed., *Ethical Issues Relating to Life and Death* (New York: Oxford University Press, 1979), especially sections II and IV.

concept of death is that of a *person's* death. Secondly, that this is the way death has always been conceived and hence what is required for the resolution of the bioethical difficulties is not a revision of the concept of death, but rather a revision of the traditional criterion of the death of a person: i.e. death of the biological organism.

One way to develop this line of thought would be to push a suggestion that seems implicit here and maintain that death should properly be equated with the extinction of a person. In other words, the suggestion that we should commit ourselves to a strong claim: viz. the identification of death with the extinction of the person, rather than the extinction of the human being. An argument for this view might be as follows.[7] Suppose we claim of a particular patient, Jones, that he is alive. In order for this to be true it must both be true that (i) the patient is alive, and (ii) the patient is (remains) Jones. If it is true that the patient, though alive, is not Jones, and if it is also true that no one else is Jones, then Jones does not exist. We have already conceded the possibility of a person's extinction predating the disintegration of a human being. Hence if we can show that Jones no longer exists, then this presumably establishes that Jones is dead, notwithstanding the continued existence of a human being (the patient). Of course, the trouble with this view is that by identifying death with the extinction of the person we will be committed to the thesis that it is analytically true that no one (i.e. no person) can survive his or her death: an unsatisfactory foreclosure of a controversial, and presumably open, question. Moreover, it also makes it analytically true that if persons do indeed survive the distintegration of their associated biological organisms, as various religions have claimed, then no one actually *dies*. But nobody — religionist or secularist — wants to claim that.

In fact Tooley's own explicit claim is weaker than this strong view. He conceives of the death of a person "either as the complete ceasing to be of a continuing subject of mental states or as the severing of all relationship between such a continuing subject and the biological organism with which it has been associated."[8] The second part of this disjunction is presumably supposed to deal with the possibility (raised by Tooley himself) of a person's memories, character etc. all being destroyed and replaced by

---

[7] Cf. Green and Wikler, pp. 117-118.

[8] Tooley, "Decisions to Terminate Life and the Concept of Person", pp. 75-76.

other desires, attitudes etc. without damage to the associated biological organism. In such an instance, Tooley maintains, the original person would no longer exist, notwithstanding the fact that the biological organism would be unaffected and moreover still associated with a continuing subject of mental states. In this case the continuing subject would be a different person from the extinguished person formerly associated with the biological organism.

As a specification of what is involved in the death of a person, this is surely unsatisfactory. It seems to rule out in advance, for example, the possibility of a person surviving as a different human being or, alternatively, surviving as a person though no longer as a human being.[9] Furthermore, on Tooley's view a person can be destroyed without the biological organism with which he is associated being destroyed simply by the expedient of destroying the person's memory and personality traits. This claim has some counterintuitive consequences. Thus Graham Oddie cites an actual case of a woman who caught a disease from a native New Zealand bird resulting in a coma from which she emerged with no memory of her previous personal history.[10] Presumably on Tooley's account her subsequent attempts to recover her sense of identity are more properly understood to be her discovering facts about a dead person and trying to establish a sense of self-identification with this deceased person. Of course, all of this depends upon how much is packed into the phrase "the severing of *all relationship* between such a continuing subject and the biological organism with which it has been associated." This is vague enough to leave the precise nature of this condition unclear. More recently Tooley has claimed that personal identity presupposes a relation of causal dependence between mental states existing at different times and hence "one property ... that a human person can lose only on pain of ceasing to be is that of standing in a certain causal relation to earlier mental occurrences." The deprogramming example is supposed to be an instance of the death of a person because there is "no causal connection, *of the appropriate sort*, between present mental events and past ones."[11] Once again, however, this causal condition is left hopelessly vague.

---

9 In *Abortion and Infanticide* (p. 161) Tooley concedes at least the latter possibility.

10 Graham Oddie, "What Should We Do With Human Embryos?" *Interchange*, forthcoming.

11 *Abortion and Infanticide*, p. 164. (My emphasis.)

What lessons should we draw from all this then? I suggest that we can usefully take over the distinction between (i) the destruction of a functioning biological organism, and (ii) the destruction of a person. My proposal is that death be identified with the former, not the latter. That is, *death* is the annihilation of a functioning biological organism, not the destruction of a person. One important argument for this is that animals *die*, even if their deaths do not involve the annihilation of any persons. (The supposition that some non-human animals are persons would not affect this point. Oysters and flies, for example, are presumably not persons, but they nevertheless die — as also do trees and flowers.) Sense (i), then, captures the concept of death that is neutral to all deaths. The disagreement between the secularist and religionist is not really (*pace* Walton) a disagreement about the concept of death: both can agree that death is the destruction of a biological organism. What their disagreement is about is whether a further thesis about death is true: viz. that the destruction of the person coincides with the destruction of the associated biological organism. In fact, even this does not entirely capture their disagreement, for both might agree that these do not coincide. Hence many religions have claimed that the person is not destroyed at death (i.e. at the destruction of the associated biological organism). Of course, the secularist denies this claim, but he may (like Tooley) want to claim that the destruction of the person need not involve the destruction of the biological organism. The important point, however, is that these disagreements are not disagreements about the concept of death. The differences which are really at issue here turn upon certain substantive metaphysical theses about the relations that actually obtain between instances of the concept of death (particularly death of a human being) and instances of the concept of the extinction of a person.

The identification of death with the destruction of a biological organism, rather than the destruction of a person, does have at least one interesting consequence. If we accept the claim that a person can cease to exist even though the associated biological organism is undamaged, then we could presumably have a situation where it is true to say that a person (Jones) no longer exists but false to say that Jones has died. Indeed the possibility of such a situation is required in order to meet the argument advanced earlier for the identification of death with destruction of a person. That argument, it will be recalled, rests on the assumption that "Jones no longer exists" entails "Jones has died". Now denying this entailment might seem a little odd at first glance, but in fact this denial is only a weakly counterintuitive consequence of my account of death. After all, suppose we admit that persons can cease to exist without their associated biological organisms ceasing to exist via the expedient of deprogramming and reprogramming. In such a case a new human person has come into existence without being conceived or born. (I assume these latter two processes are purely biological.) In the light of this there is nothing odd about human persons going out of existence without dying.

A further argument is possible here. Birth (or conception) and death are both boundary concepts: they mark the coming into being and ceasing to be of a living entity and are thus apparently symmetrical. This apparent symmetry presents us with at least a prima facie case for a symmetrical account of the two concepts. At the very least, such a symmetrical account would be a desideratum, since a unified theory is always (other things being equal) rationally preferable. But if we were to identify death with the destruction of a person then this symmetry would not obtain. This is because, as we have just seen, it seems that persons can come into existence without being born (or conceived). Hence birth (or conception) cannot be identified with the coming into existence of a person. However, if we identify death with the destruction of the biological organism, then we can correspondingly identify birth (or conception) with the coming into existence of the appropriate biological organism and satisfy the desideratum of conceptual symmetry.

Consider a different possibility. On the account sketched so far death is the destruction of a functioning biological organism, not the destruction of a person. Whether these two distinct occurrences happen to coincide will be a contingent fact about our world; the two concepts are logically discrete. Thus "Jones has died" does not entail "Jones has ceased to exist"; nor does "Jones has ceased to exist "entail "Jones has died". However, "A biological organism has died" does entail "A biological organism has ceased to exist". Does "A biological organism has ceased to exist" entail "A biological organism has died"? Apparently not. Recall the case of Gregor Samsa in Kafka's story *The Metamorphosis*. Gregor wakes up one morning to find himself transformed into a gigantic insect. The human being (i.e. the biological organism) formerly associated with Gregor has ceased to exist, though the person Gregor survives in an insect's body. Presumably we are to imagine that the human being has metamorphosed into an insect though personal identity has been preserved. In such a case a human being has ceased to exist and an insect come into existence, but no one has *died*. So it is true that a biological organism can cease to exist without it being the case that a biological organism has died. And this is surely surprising if death is the ceasing to exist of a living organism. However the phrase "the ceasing to exist of a living organism" is ambiguous between (i) X is a living organism *of a particular type* until a certain time and not a living organism of that type thereafter, and (ii) X is a living organism before a certain time and not a living organism thereafter. What the case of Gregor's metamorphosis shows is that we need to distinguish between these two senses and identify death with the latter sense. Hence a human being's ceasing to exist is not itself death, provided that it turns into another living organism. After all, when tadpoles metamorphose into frogs, or caterpillars into butterflies, no *deaths* of tadpoles or caterpillars occur. Of course, there still remain some hard metaphysical questions about identity and change. Fortunately we don't have to be in possession of all the answers to these in order to see the general sort of account that could be offered. Hence in metamorphic cases like that of Gregor's personal identity is presumably guaranteed by the presence (in various degrees) of factors like causal and spatio-temporal continuity, psychological constancy, etc. Also important in such metamorphic cases is the gradualness of the process. In the case of an instantaneous change from a tadpole to a frog we might well be tempted to insist that a tadpole *had* died and been replaced by a frog.

These metamorphic examples are also useful for providing us with a model for understanding the relations between dying and death. Dying is a process; death is an event; being dead is a state. Though the first of these three claims is indisputable, the other two are more controversial. Some, for instance, have claimed that death is a process, or even a state.[12] Let's begin, then, with the uncontroversial claim that dying

---

[12] For the first claim see Robert S. Morison, "Death: Process or Event?" in Weir, pp. 57-69. (This paper is criticized in Leon R. Kass, "Death as an Event: A Commentary on Robert Morison" in Weir, pp. 70-81.) For the second claim see Skegg, p. 186n.

is a process. What sort of a process is it? Presumably it is some sort of metamorphic process that generally ends in the disintegration of a living organism (i.e. death). Is it, however, a process that has to involve the attainment of such an end, or is it a process that need not end in death? Surely it is the latter. In other words, "die" is (in Ryle's terminology) a task-verb, not an achievement-verb: "dying" is more like "travelling" than "arriving" (at least in our world). Hence in order for it to be true that at a given time an individual is dying it is not necessary for that individual actually to complete the process and die. (This is what gives point to an imperative like: "Help me quickly — this man is dying!")[13] In this regard compare dying with other sorts of metamorphic processes. In order for it to be true, for example, that a tadpole is turning into a frog it is not necessary that the frog actually come into being — perhaps a predator eats the metamorphosing tadpole. Dying, then, is a process that if uninterrupted by external forces will normally end in death; but dying does not necessarily eventuate in death.

Death, on the other hand, I hold to be an event which marks the being/has-been boundary for living organisms. Generally it represents the completion of a process of dying. But it need not do so, for presumably a death could be instantaneous and thus not the result of any process of dying. As already mentioned, there are those who claim death to be a process, not a discrete event. Life and death are then held to be parts of a continuum and hence it must be impossible to identify a border between them. This is unconvincing. The relevant opposition here is not between death and life, but between death and birth (or conception), i.e. whatever concept symmetrically identifies an organism's coming into existence. Birth (or conception) thus marks the transition (abrupt or gradual, continuous or discontinuous) from becoming into being. This becoming is a process and the last event of the process (birth or conception) completes the whole process. Similarly, dying is a process which (if uninterrupted) ends in a transition from being to has-been. The last event of the process (death) completes this transition.

Nor should we conclude that death is a process from the fact that the various organs and systems supporting the continuation of life fail and cease to function

---

[13] Cf. Ninian Smart, "Philosophical Concepts of Death" in Toynbee *et al.*, p. 28.

successively and at different times. Death is the disintegration of the living organism *as a whole*, not its individual parts. That the disintegration of the organism as a whole (death) generally represents the completion of a process of dying does not imply that death (like dying) is a process. Death, conceived of as the disintegration of the organism as a whole, is presumably a discrete event which takes place at a particular time. Any difficulty in identifying that event will be epistemic and not the consequence of any metaphysical indeterminacy. If there is any vagueness about the time of a death it is to be located in the vagueness of the concept of a functioning living organism. Does the latter exclude, for instance, the possibility of an organism's functions being artificially sustained, as in the bioethically problematic cases mentioned earlier? The important point here, however, is that any efforts to make the concept of a functioning living organism more precise will correspondingly eliminate any apparent vagueness in the time of a death and thereby strengthen the plausibility of the claim that death is a discrete event.

Death, then, is an event (the disintegration of a living organism as a whole) that marks the transition from the state of being alive to the state of being dead. That is, it is *being dead*, not death, that is a state. Of course, the state of being dead is ontologically related to the event of death. Indeed the event of death will be the first event in the series of events that constitute the state of being dead. This is because states are ontologically reducible to series of events, as also are processes. Roughly speaking, a process is a series of events involving change within certain constraints of continuity, whereas a state is a series of events involving relative stability.

Thus there is no special difficulty involved in sketching out the elements of a general metaphysical account of the concept of death as the disintegration of a living organism. And it is important to insist that this concept is quite distinct from the concept of the destruction of a person. But how does this metaphysical account then bear upon the legal and bioethical issues of death and dying? It is clear enough that one set of contemporary worries about the medical and legal definition of death are really just worries about the use of new criteria for determining whether the old concept of death has been instantiated. The resolution of these worries will in turn depend partly upon advances in the science of medicine and partly upon juristic stipulation. However the elimination of that sort of difficulty would do nothing to resolve many of the troublesome bioethical problems about when to permit organ transplants, when to turn off respirators, etc. And this is hardly surprising. It would be naive to imagine that science and logic can answer all the questions of ethics. Take any patient in one of the ethically problematic states: the moral questions about what it is permissible to do to a patient in such a state will still arise however that state is designated. Definitions of death cannot define away the moral problems.

Nevertheless there still remain those who feel that since our concerns with the definition of death are generated by moral concerns, we are justified in allowing our value commitments to guide our judgements about the acceptability of proposed definitions (or redefinitions). Jonathan Glover is explicit about this. He proposes that "death" should be defined in terms of irreversible loss of consciousness. In defence of what he acknowledges to be a proposal for conceptual reform, he says:

> The only way of choosing [between competing definitions of death] is to decide whether or not we attach any value to the preservation of someone irreversibly comatose. Do we value "life" even if unconscious, or do we value life only as a vehicle for consciousness?[14]

This is hardly acceptable. Of course, it is true enough that there are complex relations between our choice of a categorical scheme and our value commitments. However, if a warrior culture values the martial virtues so exclusively that the mode of existence of those unfitted for the warrior life is thought to be worthless, it does not follow that they are justified in reclassifying such non-warriors as *dead*.[15] The ontological status of such non-warriors is quite distinct from evaluations of their mode of being.

The central point of all this, then, is that we must not suppose that medicine, or law, or even metaphysics, can by themselves dissolve those troublesome ethical problems about, for instance, when it is permissible to terminate medical care. Of

---

[14] Jonathan Glover, *Causing Death and Saving Lives* (Harmondsworth: Penguin, 1977), p. 45.

[15] Cf. Green and Wikler, p. 116 for a similar point.

course, this is not to deny that medicine, law and metaphysics can be relevant for guiding our decisions on these ethical questions. But it is important to understand that the task of defining death is not itself a moral task, even though much of our interest in the project may be generated by puzzlement about the bioethical issues.

So far I have offered a general metaphysical account of death as the disintegration of a biological organism, rather than the destruction of a person. This account is neutral with respect to the question of whether we survive death and in at least this regard is surely closer to the traditional concept of death than rival accounts that claim death is the destruction of persons. I have also tried to distinguish the metaphysical questions about death from bioethical questions like, "When is it permissible to terminate medical care?" I now want to conclude this chapter with some remarks about the epistemic status of our knowledge of death.

Douglas Walton has suggested that there is an inverted analogy between some epistemic properties of death and the traditional philosophical problem of other minds. For just as my mode of epistemic access to my own private mental states seems quite different from my mode of epistemic access to the mental states of others, so too my death is my own and cannot be undergone by any subject other than myself. The analogy is inverted because (at least on the secular conception of death) "I cannot experience my own being-dead, but you, as an observer, can witness my death or being-dead."[16] Thus my own death is epistemically inaccessible to me through first-hand observation. However, Walton resists the conclusion that we can therefore know nothing whatever about death by urging a parallel with "reasonable inferences" about the mental states of others in the absence of direct access to those states. Nevertheless, on Walton's view I do seem to have to choose between the secular and religious conceptions of death in the face of a lack of any direct relevant evidence.

Now there are certain well known philosophical difficulties with the reasonableness of "reasonable inferences" to the mental states of others. This is particularly true if Walton has in mind a parallel with the argument from analogy for the existence of other minds. In other words, something like the following argument. In the case of other minds, I observe the correlations between my behaviour and my

---

[16] Walton, p. 47.

own mental states and then generalize from this to the conclusion that similar behaviour by other beings is correlated with similar mental states; in the case of death, I observe the deaths of others and infer from my physical similarity to other beings that my own death will occur, despite my inability to experience it directly. The success of this inverted analogical argument clearly depends upon the reasonableness of the first inference. But it would be tendentious to assure us that the second part of the argument is sound because of its parallel to the first part of the argument. This is because the first part (the argument from analogy for the existence of other minds) is itself open to serious objection. In the first place, construed as an inductive generalization from a single case the analogical argument for other minds is inherently weak; indeed far too weak to warrant our customary degree of confidence in the existence of other minds. Secondly, presumably I can only properly be justified in ascribing to others mental states very similar to my own. But then my tone-deafness and colour-blindness should make it unreasonable for me to suppose that others have different auditory and visual sensations to me. Finally, the analogical argument can only be defensible if it is possible, at least in principle, to determine independently that the fourth term exists. However, in the case of other minds there is, *ex hypothesi*, no such possibility.

On the other hand, if death is conceived of as the disintegration of a biological organism (a human being, for instance), then some of these epistemic difficulties about death disappear. Firstly, we can rid ourselves of Walton's worries about having to choose between the secular and the religious conceptions of death in the absence of direct relevant evidence. The account I am offering involves only one conception of death and that is in itself neutral between differing secular and religious expectations about personal survival. Whether persons survive death (i.e. the disintegration of their associated biological organisms) is a quite distinct matter from the question of what death is, and it is a piece of metaphysical gerrymandering to try to build an answer to the latter question into the concept of death itself.

Secondly, while I certainly agree that we can have knowledge of the deaths of others, since we can obviously observe the disintegration of their associated biological organisms, on my view of death it remains an open question as to whether I can have direct knowledge of my own death. This is because the real issue in dispute here is whether the destruction of the person generally coincides with the disintegration of the biological organism (i.e. death). If it does, then perhaps it is true that I will not be able to have direct knowledge of my own death; if it does not, then presumably I will be able to have direct knowledge of my own death. Hence in the case of the deaths of others I can have direct knowledge of their deaths, while in the case of my own death I can have direct knowledge of it provided that it does not coincide with my destruction as a person. Of course, if the events of my death and my extinction as a person do coincide, then I may not be able to have direct knowledge of my own death. But the hypothesis that I will die is at least *possibly* subject to verification by me. And in this respect the analogy with the problem of other minds breaks down.

Is there perhaps at least an inverted analogy between the problem of other minds and our knowledge, not of death, but of the destruction of persons? Much depends here on how we construe key terms like "direct knowledge" and "person". In each case a strong or a weak construal is possible. Thus on a strong construal of "direct knowledge" it would be trivially true that no one but the subject of an experience can have direct knowledge of that experience: compare the trivial truth that you cannot have direct knowledge of *my* toothache because you are not (and cannot be) *me*. A weak construal of "direct knowledge", however, would allow for the possibility of direct knowledge of things other than our own experiences. Similarly, there is a strong construal of "person" such that a person is not merely a subject of experience, but also the possessor of certain additional person-making properties (however they are delineated). A weak construal of "person", however, identifies the term simply with "sentient being". These distinct senses of "direct knowledge" and "person" in turn permit four possible combinations. Do any of them yield an inverted analogy with the problem of other minds?

The first possibility is to take strong construals both of "direct knowledge" and "person". In this case I cannot have direct knowledge of the destruction of other persons but I can have direct knowledge of my own destruction as a person. After all, subjects of experience can presumably survive the destruction of themselves as persons (in the strong sense): not all sentient creatures capable of direct knowledge are usually held to be persons, as the weak sense of "person" requires. Thus if X is a person who ceases to be a person, though surviving as a sentient being of a sufficient degree of epistemic sophistication, then X has direct experience of the destruction of herself as a person. Compare the tadpole which metamorphoses into a frog. The resultant frog can (at least in principle) have direct knowledge of the destruction of himself as a tadpole. Hence on the strong construals of "direct knowledge" and "person" I (as a subject of experience) can presumably have direct knowledge of my destruction as a person, but not direct knowledge of the destruction of other persons. But in that case there is no *inverted* analogy with the problem of other minds; rather there is a direct analogue.

The second possibility is to construe "direct knowledge" strongly and "person" weakly. On such a construal I can only have direct knowledge of my own experiences, while "person" means merely "subject of experience". Thus in this case I cannot have direct knowledge of the destruction of other persons, but neither can I have direct knowledge of my own destruction as a person (i.e. a sentient being). In other words, there is not the epistemic asymmetry an analogy with the other minds problem requires.

The third possibility is to construe "direct knowledge" weakly and "person" strongly. In this case I can then have direct knowledge of the destruction of other persons, but I can also have direct knowledge of my own destruction as a person. That is, once again there is no epistemic asymmetry and hence no analogy with the other minds problem.

The fourth and final possibility is to construe both "direct knowledge" and "person" weakly. In this case I can have direct knowledge of the destruction of other persons but not of my own destruction as a person (i.e. a sentient being). And here we do have a kind of inverted analogy with the other minds problem.

Only the first and last combinations, then, yield an analogy with the other minds problem. The first combination, however, presents us with a direct analogue with the other minds problem, not an inverted analogy. Moreover, in order to generate the analogy we have to construe "direct knowledge" so strongly that the only direct knowledge we can have is of our own experiences. This construal is unattractive. Surely we do have, in a quite unproblematic sense, direct knowledge of things other than our own experiences — including perhaps events like the destruction of other persons. Of course, it is true that if we weakly construe "direct knowledge" and combine it with a weak construal of "person" then we can generate a kind of inverted analogy with the other minds problem. (This is the fourth possibility considered above.) However, in the first place the sense of "direct knowledge" appealed to here is much weaker than the sense required for the original other minds problem to arise; and in the second place, the sense of "person" is so weak as to trivialize the point being made.

But there does nevertheless remain a different, though related, problem which has not yet been touched upon. Even if our knowledge of our own deaths is epistemically on a par with our knowledge of the deaths of others, there still is arguably a problem about the special nature of our consciousness of our own deaths *for us*. This difficulty is rather like a familiar worry in the philosophy of mind: the phenomenological qualitative character of an experience *for the subject* seems to be left out of an objective, third-person account of consciousness. Similarly for death: my mode of consciousness of my own death is *for me* of a different sort from my consciousness of the deaths of others. Any attempt to reduce it to the same type as my consciousness of others' deaths simply fails to capture this important difference. I believe that the assessment of this argument requires us to consider more closely a very interesting and difficult problem, one which will occupy our attention in the next chapter.

CHAPTER 2: "MY DEATH"

I

The belief that the notion of one's own death is somehow problematic is a widespread one, quite apart from any purported analogy with the other minds problem. It is frequently supposed, for example, that there is some special difficulty involved in a person's attempt to conceive of or imagine his or her own death. Indeed it is sometimes maintained that I *cannot* conceive of or imagine my own death (where "I" and "my" refer, of course, to the person attempting this supposedly impossible task). What is supposed to follow from this claim is by no means obvious, though Goethe is reported to have inferred his immortality from his inability to conceive of the termination of his own consciousness. Moreover this alleged inconceivability is also often proposed as a source of the fear of death. That is, I try to conceive of my own death and cannot. The result is a fear of "nothingness" or "the void". At least two sorts of argument have been advanced for such a view of the inconceivability of one's own death.

The first argument maintains that when we try to imagine our own deaths we smuggle in the continued existence of ourselves as spectators who remain to do the imagining, for indeed we cannot do anything else. As Freud puts it:

It is indeed impossible to imagine our own death; and whenever we attempt to do so we can perceive that we are in fact still present as spectators.[1]

The second argument (of Heideggerian pedigree) claims that in statements about one's own death the word "death" has a different meaning to what it does in statements about the deaths of others, for with my death my world comes to an end and this is not so with the deaths of others.

---

[1] Sigmund Freud, "Thoughts for the Times on War and Death" in *The Standard Edition of the Complete Psychological Works of Sigmund Freud*, Vol. 14 (London: Hogarth Press, 1957), p. 289. Compare also Ramchandra Gandhi, *The Availability of Religious Ideas* (London: Macmillan, 1976), p. 39.

From the point of view of the analysis of death offered in the previous chapter these arguments are both unsatisfactory since they identify death with the cessation of the conscious individual. Neither argument will show that it is impossible for me to conceive of my own death if we accept the already offered account of death as the disintegration of a biological organism. Can these arguments be reformulated, however, to establish that we cannot conceive of our own (permanent) extinction as sentient beings? After all, it may still happen that (as some maintain) our deaths coincide with our cessation as conscious beings, in which case the reformulated arguments may establish some property of an event constantly conjoined with death. But even so reconstrued the arguments are unconvincing. Paul Edwards, for example, while ingenuously identifying death with the cessation of the conscious individual, nevertheless sharply criticizes the two arguments in question.[2] In the first place he maintains that the trivial sense in which I am a spectator in all my thoughts just because I am thinking them implies nothing about my appearing as (in that sense) a spectator in them. Furthermore, since it is conceded that someone else *can* conceive of my death, what is the other thinking of that I cannot think of? Suppose that we concede that my death is the dissolution of my body and the cessation of my experiences. But if the fact that this other person is alive when thinking of my death doesn't disqualify him from thinking of this, then why should my being alive prevent me from thinking of this either? Moreover, if it is admitted that we can conceive of our nonexistence before our birth, why is there no problem here when there is supposed to be one about the conceiving of our own nonexistence after death?

In the second place Edwards denies that "death" in "my death" means anything different. True, my attitude to my death will be differently charged emotionally for me than my attitude to the deaths of others. But the same is true of my attitude to being a father. It doesn't thereby follow that "father" used of myself means something different to "father" used of another. Further, though we can understand why some-one might want to say something like "With my death, my world comes to an end", this doesn't imply that with death *the* world comes to an end — even if it is true that at

---

[2] Paul Edwards, 'My Death' in Paul Edwards, ed., *The Encyclopedia of Philosophy*, Vol. 5 (New York: Macmillan, 1967), pp. 416-419.

death my experience of *the* world does come to an end. Finally, the fact that (if we identify death with the cessation of the conscious individual) I can witness the deaths of others but not my own doesn't show that "death" means something different in the two cases. Neither can I experience another being's pain or pleasure, but that doesn't entail that "pain" and "pleasure" have different meanings when applied to me and to others.

Edwards' conclusions are summed up by him thus:

> For in whatever sense or senses the deaths of others and the nonexistence of oneself before birth can be conceived, in precisely this sense or senses can the death of oneself also be both imagined and conceived.[3]

And it seems to me that what Edwards says in this sentence is indeed true. However, I want to argue that if we try to fill out these "sense or senses" we come to see that there is more to be said for the view that Edwards is criticizing than he seems to allow. Indeed to investigate the conceptual oddities of "my death" is to encounter another instance of a familiar philosophical tension between subjective and objective points of view.

II

In an influential but difficult passage in *Being and Time* (sect. 47), Heidegger argues that we cannot succeed in understanding our own deaths on the model of our understanding of the deaths of others. It might seem that since we see others die and we assume that they are essentially like ourselves, all we have to do is extend our analysis of the deaths of others to include our own case. Heidegger, however, rejects this claim that we can come to understand our own deaths through such an understanding of others' deaths:

> ... we have no way of access to the loss-of-Being as such which the dying man 'suffers'. The dying of Others is not something which we can experience in a genuine sense; at most we are always just 'there alongside'.

---

[3] Ibid., p. 417.

And even if, by thus Being there alongside, it were possible and feasible for us to make plain to ourselves 'psychologically' the dying of Others, this would by no means grasp the way-to-be which we would then have in mind — namely, coming-to-an-end. We are asking about the ontological meaning of the dying of the person who dies, as a possibility-of-Being which belongs to *his* Being.[4]

This jargon-freighted passage is likely to strike an analytic philosopher as unnecessarily opaque. The temptation is to reduce Heidegger's claim either to triviality or to falsehood.[5] Someone might want to argue, for instance, that Heidegger is guilty of an equivocation. Thus there is a sense in which it is trivially true that I cannot have direct access to your experience of your own dying, if by that it is merely meant that it is logically impossible for *me* to have *your* experiences. However, this does not imply that there is not another sense in which I do have access to your experiences. And it is this sort of access to your dying that I may use to understand my own dying. (Compare in this regard our earlier discussion of alleged analogies between our knowledge of death and our knowledge of other minds.)

This brisk treatment, however, surely does not do justice to Heidegger's point. It seems to me that a more plausible interpretation of his view is that he is claiming that there is a first-person, subjective perspective on death that cannot be adequately captured by a third-person, objective perspective. In other words, that the significance *for me* of the expression "I will die" cannot be analysed exhaustively into a purely third-person reading of "This body will cease to function and will decay". This is because my death is not *for me* an occurrence in the world in the way another's death is. For myself, I am not *in* the world as another is.[6]

---

[4] Martin Heidegger, *Being and Time*, trans. John Macquarrie and Edward Robinson (London: SCM Press, 1962), p. 282-283.

[5] For a typically unsympathetic treatment of Heidegger's views by an analytic philosopher see Paul Edwards, *Heidegger on Death: A Critical Evaluation* (La Salle: Hegeler Institute, 1979).

[6] My interpretation here has been influenced by two papers of William H. Poteat's: see his "Birth, Suicide and the Doctrine of Creation: An Exploration of Analogies" and "'I Will Die': An Analysis" in D. Z. Phillips, ed., *Religion and Understanding* (Oxford: Basil Blackwell, 1967), pp. 127-139, 199-213.

Thus construed Heidegger's claim should no longer seem unfamiliar to an analytic philosopher, despite his unfamiliar terminology. The idea that there exists a conceptual tension between the subjective, internal point of view of individual human life and the objective, external conception of reality is, for example, a central concern of Thomas Nagel's recent philosophical work.[7] Hence in his *Mortal Questions* Nagel groups together a number of apparently disparate traditional philosophical problems (mind-body, personal identity, free will, etc.) in order to present them as illustrative of a general thesis about the subjective and the objective. This thesis is that there is an ineliminable opposition between subjective and objective points of view. And this in turn presents us with the problem of the relative priority of two ways of looking at the world: the objective viewpoint that tells us the way things are in themselves and the subjective viewpoint that tells us the way things are from the perspective of a subject who apprehends them.

If the analogy I am drawing here is sound then the Heideggerian claim is presumably that my death cannot just be viewed by me in the manner in which I view others' deaths. This is because the subjective, internal viewpoint from which I view my own death is not the same as the objective viewpoint from which I view others' deaths; nor is the subjective viewpoint eliminable or reducible to the objective viewpoint.

With regard to death William Poteat has argued that this conceptual distinction is highlighted by a linguistic point:

> It makes perfectly good sense for me to sensibly say, "Jones is dying", "Jones has died", or "Jones will die". I cannot sensibly say: "I died". This verb cannot be meaningfully conjugated in the past tense, first person singular — or, if it is, it cannot be used.[8]

---

[7] Thomas Nagel, *Mortal Questions* (Cambridge: Cambridge University Press, 1979), especially Ch. 14. See also his "The Limits of Objectivity" in Sterling M. McMurrin, ed., *The Tanner Lectures on Human Values*, Vol. 1 (Salt Lake City: University of Utah Press, 1980), pp. 77-139.

[8] Poteat, "'I Will Die': An Analysis", p. 204.

This claim, however, is highly dubious. Consider the case of the ancient Middle Eastern Order of Assassins as reported in *The Travels of Marco Polo*.[9] The leader of this sect, Marco records, constructed an amazing garden after the description of Paradise in the *Koran*. He would then drug youths into unconsciousness and place them in the garden. When they awoke, "simple mountain folk" that they were, they believed that they had died and been transported to the Paradise of their holy text. When the Sheikh required an emissary to send on a mission of assassination he would drug one of these youths again and carry him out of the garden into his palace. The youth would awake and naturally regret his fall from Paradise. He would tell others of the the splendours of Paradise so they too "longed for death so that they might go there, and looked forward eagerly to the day of their going." The Sheikh would then send the young Assassin on a murderous mission with the promise that he (a great prophet) would dispatch him to Paradise on his successful return, or if he died on the mission he would go there all the sooner. Now such a youth, awakening in the paradisial garden, could quite naturally say, "Last night I died and now I am in Paradise." This statement would, in fact, be false but it is entirely meaningful and the youth can certainly use such an expression. (Indeed, given the context, it seems quite a reasonable thing to say.) Thus Poteat's "grammatical" argument apparently fails.

In order for Poteat's argument to go through it must be that by "death" he means "the cessation of the individual". I have already argued against such an account of death in the previous chapter and it is perhaps a merit of my alternative account of death that it can accommodate the intuitively attractive claim that the young Assassin's statement is (*contra* Poteat) a perfectly significant utterance. My account can also accommodate that long tradition in Western thought which would regard death as only the cessation of the *physical* individual.[10] After all, it may be that what we ordinarily identify as cases of death actually involve only *bodily* disintegration, in which instance there would remain a possible use for "I died". Anyway, even if death is conceived of

---

[9] *The Travels of Marco Polo*, trans. Ronald Latham (Harmondsworth: Penguin, 1958), pp. 39-42. An excellent historical study of the Order is Bernard Lewis, *The Assassins* (London: Weidenfeld and Nicolson, 1967).

[10] Ninian Smart criticizes Poteat for ignoring this tradition in his *Philosophers and Religious Truth* 2nd ed. (London: SCM Press, 1969), pp. 168-170.

as the cessation of the individual, this is apparently compatible with another traditional eschatological option: the possibility of resurrection. To rule out this possibility Poteat would have to commit himself to a strong definition of death as "the *permanent* cessation of the individual". Now if this is what death is then (analytically) no individual can survive it. However, in the first place it is surely unhappy to circumscribe so the concept of death that it becomes merely tautologous to assert that there is no life after death. Secondly, even if we do decide to circumscribe the concept of death in this manner, it still remains an open question whether anyone "dies". In other words, nothing interesting about the irreducibility of a first-person account of my death to a third-person account will follow from such a conception of death. The point about "I died" lacking a (first-person) use will just be a point about the pragmatics of such utterances. On this account of death the proposition "I died" will be like the proposition "I do not exist". In both cases though the proposition itself is not self-refuting, any assertion of it is.

Mackie has classified such examples as instances of "operational self-refutation". In such cases we find that:

> The only possible way of presenting the item is to "coherently assert" it, and since this involves asserting something that conflicts with the item itself, this precise item cannot be presented at all. And yet what is in a sense an equivalent item can be presented (say by another speaker) and may be true.[11]

Of course, essential to Poteat's position is the claim that "I died" and "Roy Perrett died" are not really equivalents (at least for me). However it is worth noting that even if Poteat's claim is true, this irreducibility will not in itself demonstrate anything about my prospects of immortality. The fact that I cannot coherently assert "I died" (where that is equivalent to "I do not exist") does not in itself show that the proposition asserted is false. Compare in this regard "I believe nothing", which is also operationally self-refuting. Although it is true that I cannot myself coherently assert that I believe nothing, it may yet in fact be true that I believe nothing.

---

[11] J. L. Mackie, "Self-refutation — A Formal Analysis" *Philosophical Quarterly* **14** (1964): 197.

III

Nevertheless, there surely still is something in the claim that "I will die" cannot be exhaustively analysed into a purely third-person reading, despite the failure of Poteat's grammatical argument for this. Recall again Nagel's distinction between the subjective and objective viewpoints on reality. Presumably if it is the case that the subjective viewpoint on one's own death cannot be captured by the objective viewpoint, then this will be a special case of Nagel's general thesis about the tension between subjective and objective. It is, however, worth clarifying exactly what this general thesis is. Clearly Nagel believes that the objective appoach yields only a partial account of reality. But this claim admits of both strong and weak construals.[12] The weak thesis is that the objective approach gives an incomplete picture and requires supplementation by the subjective approach. The strong thesis is that the objective approach actually conflicts with the subjective approach and this conflict is not rationally resolvable. Nagel is apparently committed to the strong thesis; but even the weak thesis would serve to support a claim that one's own death cannot be completely grasped from the objective standpoint.

On the other hand, if one wants to deny the importance of the subjective and insist that reality is limited to the objective, then there are (as Nagel points out) basically three options open with respect to the subjective: viz. reduction, elimination and annexation. In other words, the anti-subjectivist can try to reduce all subjective appearances to corresponding objective features; or he can simply eliminate the subjective viewpoint as illusory; or he can posit some further objective entity (e.g. the ego, the will, etc.) which annexes the recalcitrant subjective element to the objective world. For Nagel, however, none of these strategies is convincing. Annexation is unsatisfactory because the very same problems of subjectivity will arise for the newly posited objective category. Reduction is also unsatisfactory in that such analyses too often fail to capture convincingly the subjective quality that gives rise to the problem. (Consider, for example, the widespread dissatisfaction with the failure of the causal theory of mind to accommodate phenomenal properties of mental states.) Finally, just

---

[12] Cf. Vinit Haksar, "Nagel on Subjective and Objective" *Inquiry* **24** (1981): 105-121.

to ignore the subjective dimension altogether and dismiss it as illusory seems to go against intuitions at least as strong as those that underpin the objective viewpoint.

But what alternatives are left to us if we reject all of these three strategies? Nagel's own position is that the subjective and objective viewpoints are each ineliminable and yet in conflict with each other. Thus he proposes that we admit the coexistence of conflicting points of view, with no rational means of resolving the clash available to us. In other words, a self-avowedly romantic espousal of "pluralistic discord" and, ultimately, irrationalism. To avoid this irrationalism and yet admit the irreducibility of both the subjective and objective viewpoints we have to deny that the subjective and objective actually conflict. That is, when such an apparent clash arises it must be that one viewpoint is mistaken (though, we may have difficulty determining which one it is that is at fault).[13] But this weaker position amounts to an espousal of one of the three strategies rejected by Nagel: viz. elimination. In order to avoid irrationalism the possibility of genuine conflict is ruled out. However, in order to do this we have to hold that prima facie conflicts can be resolved by plausibly denying the claims of either the subjective or the objective viewpoint. Given that the subjective and objective viewpoints are held to be irreducible to each other, then the weak claim is equivalent to saying that (at least in some cases) one viewpoint is eliminable as illusory.

Well, why not say this? Because to be willing so to reject as illusory one of the competing viewpoints in such a case seems to commit us to the legitimacy of a policy of deliberately suppressing intuitions if we should choose to, intuitions at least as strong as those which favour the opposing viewpoint. And this possibility in turn highlights some very fundamental metaphilosophical questions about the status of intuitions and their significance for the evaluation of our theories about reality.

Nagel's unwillingness to ignore the subjective viewpoint stems from an unwillingness to ignore our intuitions about this dimension of reality. The implicit (and widespread) conception of philosophy that underpins this unwillingness holds that philosophical theories are obliged to do justice to our intuitions. On this conception of philosophy to suppress some intuitions because they do not square with a favoured theory is as intellectually dishonest as to suppress experimental data which is incom-

---

[13] This is Haksar's position.

patible with a favoured scientific theory. Of course, if it turns out that our intuitions
on some matter are inconsistent then we have two alternatives open to us. Firstly, we
might just (with Nagel) admit reality to contain such inconsistencies. Secondly, we
might maintain that the preferable theory is that which (other things being equal)
saves the greatest number of intuitions. There is arguably a parallel with scientific
methodology here. Just as a powerful scientific theory can admit some observational
anomolies; so too can a philosophical theory admit some counterintuitive consequences, provided that it captures more intuitions than any rival theory. This position
may then be supplemented by a distinction between intuitive judgements of different
generality and a methodological principle to the effect that, in general, low-level
intuitive judgements are to be given precedence over higher-level judgements.[14] (The
principle of non-contradiction should then be held, of course, to be an absolutely basic
low-level intuitive judgement, the preservation of which warrants our ignoring other,
less basic, intuitions. For it is implausible to regard non-contradiction as a high-level
general principle based upon basic intuitions about individual cases, since it conflicts
with the basic intuitions of paraconsistentists about individual cases of, for instance,
motion.[15])

     This second kind of approach can thus avoid Nagel's kind of irrationalism.
However, there still remains the knotty problem of how to decide which intuitions are
more basic than others. Moreover, presumably on this account we could have incompatible competing theories, each of which is compatible with our most basic intuitions
and each of which incorporates an equally large but non-overlapping set of higher-
level intuitions. How could we make a principled rational choice between two such
theories?

     Opposed to the sort of conception of the status of intuitions in philosophical
inquiry that we have just been considering is another one altogether.[16] On this other
view one can acknowledge the existence of intuitions (even low-level ones) that are

---

[14] Cf. Graham Oddie, *Likeness to Truth* (Dordrecht: D. Reidel, 1986), pp. 5-10.

[15] Cf. Graham Priest, "Inconsistencies in Motion" *American Philosophical Quarterly* **22** (1985):
339-346.

[16] For a good example of a vigorous statement of such a view see Richard Rorty, *Consequences of
Pragmatism* (Brighton: Harvester Press, 1982), especially pp. xxix-xxxvii.

incompatible with a given philosophical theory and yet justifiably choose to ignore them in favour of the theory. Intuitions are thus held to be no more basic than theories; indeed intuitions are held to embody inchoate theories and as such are as conjectural as the higher-level theories which may conflict with them. Of course, it is a consequence of such a view that choices between rival theories can no longer be justified in terms of how well the theories capture our intuitions. The intuitive judgement is no longer accorded any special status; in a clash between a theory and an intuition there is nothing objectionable in rejecting either one in favour of the other.

But now we once again encounter the problem of how it can be possible to adjudicate rationally between competing philosophical theories. The picture offered earlier was that low-level intuitions control philosophical theorizing in a manner similar to the way in which observation statements control scientific theorizing. If we abandon this picture, then what controls on philosophical theorizing do we have left? The supporter of this second sort of view we are considering is likely to reply to this query by advocating a pragmatic relativism at the metaphilosophical level.[17] Consider philosophical theories as like maps: different map projections of the world contain different distortions (i.e. each projection will ignore some distinction which may be reflected in another projection). But there is no one projection that is the "true" projection, though for different purposes one projection may be much more useful than another. Thus, for example, a map that is useful for reflecting relative sizes of land masses may be much more awkward than an alternative projection if one is interested in navigating a ship. In other words, it is our purposes that provide a criterion of relevance for mapping. What is an appropriate projection for a particular purpose is one which adequately translates into map-terms those judgements about which we care. That it distorts the others is of no importance, since they are not relevant to our purpose and hence we have no need of them.[18]

---

[17] Nelson Goodman advocates such a high-level relativism (under certain constraints of "rightness") in his *Ways of Worldmaking* (Brighton: Harvester Press, 1978) and *Of Mind and Other Matters* (Cambridge, Mass.: Harvard University Press, 1984).

[18] This analogy with mapping is borrowed from Karl H. Potter, *Presuppositions of India's Philosophies* (Englewood Cliffs, N. J.: Prentice-Hall, 1963), p. 29. Compare also Nelson Goodman's use of a similar analogy in his *Problems and Projects* (Indianapolis: Bobbs-Merrill, 1972), pp. 15-18.

This line of argument, however, is likely to be resisted on the following grounds. The supposed difficulty with Nagel's intuitive realism was that it led to irrationalism. Similarly, even a modified intuitive realism was claimed to be unable to provide for rational choice between certain kinds of competing theories. On the other hand, the alternative now offered to us is an anti-realistic relativism. On this view the adequacy of theories is no longer even partially constrained by faithfulness to our intuitions; rather the adequacy of theories is held to be relative to our purposes and goals. But then it seems there can be no rational choice between different theories, each of which is adequate to a given purpose. In other words, we seem to face a dilemma between (i) some variety of intuitive realism and hence, ultimately, irrationalism; or (ii) an anti-realist relativism which just introduces a similar irrationalism into the picture at a higher metaphilosophical level.

As with most dilemmas, it may be that some are satisfied to embrace one horn or the other. Hence the intuitive realist may just accept the consequence of an ineliminable irrationalism as an unavoidable fact about the world. Similarly, the anti-realist may not flinch from the relativistic consequences of his view. However, if we are unwilling to take either course then we must look for another way out. The possibility that I want to explore involves denying that the consequences of adopting the pragmatic view of the adequacy of theories are necessarily as drastic as the objection offered in the previous paragraph assumes.

The objection in question was that if we hold that the adequacy of theories is, like the adequacy of maps, to be measured in terms of their success relative to our purposes, then there can be no rational choice between conflicting theories, each of which is adequate to particular but differing purposes. Given the obvious variety of possible purposes, each generating its own map, we are committed to an extreme and unpalatable relativism. This objection, however, rests upon a crucial presupposition: viz. that there is no objective hierarchy of purposes. But someone who denies that there is any one map that will capture all the features people care about relative to all of their different purposes is not thereby committed to denying that there is some ultimate value in a hierarchy of values and purposes. Such an ultimate value will be, of course, itself a purpose and it will generate its own map which, like other maps, selects and distorts; but this does not affect its supremacy. The map generated by this ultimate value will not be the supreme map because it captures every detail that is captured by every other map projection, nor necessarily because it captures more of these than any other map. Rather it will be the supreme map because it captures every feature relevant to the purpose that is the ultimate value.

In fact the position just sketched is very much like the view common to classical Indian philosophy.[19] Traditionally Indian philosophy acknowledges a number of objective intrinsic values, but they are hierarchically arranged with liberation (*mokṣa*) as the supreme value.[20] Thus although classical Indian epistemologists tend to assess divergent theories in terms of "workability" (*pramāṇya*), the spectre of relativism fails to arise for them because of their shared conviction that there is an ultimate value. Of course, this position is unlikely to be attractive to many contemporary Western philosophers due to the widespread acceptance of noncognitivism in the theory of value. Such philosophers are not merely unwilling to admit the existence of an ultimate value, they may be unwilling even to admit that value judgements are rationally justifiable. Clearly such a view is stronger than the weak claim that there is a problem about securing agreement as to the ultimate purpose and the subsidiary goals leading to it; rather noncognitivism implies that we may not even be able to address this problem rationally. It is worth remembering, however, that this kind of noncognitivism about value, though at present widely accepted, is very much a recent phenomenon. It represents not only an important divergence in thinking between modern Western and classical Indian philosophy, but also an important divergence between modern and classical Western philosophy. The rejection of belief in an absolute value is just a consequence of this common contemporary rejection of any objective values.

The question of whether there are any convincing arguments for rejecting the belief in objective values is one that I intend to look more closely at in a moment.

---

[19] As Karl Potter has pointed out: see his *Presuppositions of India's Philosophies*, p. 30; and "Does Indian Epistemology Concern Justified True Belief?" *Journal of Indian Philosophy* 12 (1984): 307-327 (especially pp. 322-325).

[20] On classical Indian philosophy of value see particularly M. Hiriyanna, *Indian Conception of Values* (Mysore: Kavyalaya Publishers, 1975).

However, it may be as well first to recap briefly the argument so far. The original problem was about the status of intuitions (as, for example, those about the subjective) and particularly the degree to which they should control our philosophical theorizing. One proposed answer supports some form of intuitive realism: theories are constrained by intuitions and, other things being equal, should try to capture all (or at least as many as possible) of our intuitions. Another answer refuses to give intuitions any special status. On this view the adequacy of philosophical theories is not to be measured in terms of their ability to capture successfully our intuitions. Rather, theories (like maps) can legitimately ignore or distort features of our experience in the pursuit of particular purposes. The first view seems to lead ultimately to some sort of irrationalism; but the second view seems to lead to complete relativism. I argued, however, that this extreme relativism can be mitigated by admitting the objective existence of an ultimate value. Such a view will not be compatible with the popular present day support for noncognitivism about values. But it may be that without this move we will be caught either in irrationalism or in sceptical relativism. Given that both horns of the dilemma are unwelcome, it is worth exploring the way out that I have mentioned. A necessary (though not sufficient) condition for establishing the plausibility of such a view will be to show that there are no conclusive arguments against the traditional belief in objective values.

IV

A familiar metaethical typology opposes noncognitivism to cognitivism. The latter is in turn divided into naturalism and non-naturalism (or intuitionism). Noncognitivism may then be characterized as a position which denies that value judgements are true or false and in this respect is said to be in opposition to cognitivism. Naturalism and non-naturalism are said to be cognitivist theories because, though they may differ on *how* value judgements are known to be true, they both believe that value judgements are true or false. Most traditional Western theories about value are cognitivist in this sense. Moreover, the majority of these traditional theories assert the existence of objective values. This is as true of naturalistic theories like those of Aristotle, Bentham and Mill as it is of non-naturalist theories like those of Plato and the eighteenth century "moral sense" theorists; where they differ is on whether value is a natural or non-natural property (i.e. whether value terms can be defined in factual terms). However, it is nevertheless possible to be a cognitivist about value and yet deny the existence of objective values. A recent case in point is that of John Mackie.[21] According to Mackie's "error theory" value judgements have truth values all right; but as a matter of fact all value judgements are false (or at least such as we have no reason to believe them true). This is because value judgements can only be true if there are objective values and according to the error theory there are no such values (or at least no reason to believe that they exist).

Mackie's scepticism about the existence of objective values provides us with a convenient example of this widespread view, even if his error theory is, strictly speaking, not a noncognitivist one. Mackie offers two sorts of arguments against objective values: the argument from relativity and the argument from queerness.[22] The argument from relativity builds upon the the point that there seems to exist a considerable variation in moral codes from society to society, and even from individual to individual. It is then claimed that such variation is best explained not as the result of the disagreeing parties having inadequate information, but rather as the result of their participating in and adhering to differing ways of life which prevail in different communities.

The argument from queerness has two parts: one metaphysical, one epistemological. The metaphysical part is to do with the apparent ontological peculiarity of objective values. If objective values do exist, then they surely must be very queer sorts of entities, quite unlike anything else. Hence, for example, if there really are objective moral standards, then any wrong action must have its "not-to-be-doneness" somehow built into it. Again, if there is some objective property of goodness inhering in an object, then how can this be related to the natural features of that object? Suppose an

---

[21] J. L. Mackie, "A Refutation of Morals" *Australasian Journal of Philosophy and Psychology* **24** (1946): 77-90; and *Ethics: Inventing Right and Wrong* (Harmondsworth: Penguin, 1977), Ch. 1. For criticism of this error theory see Jonathan Harrison, "Mackie's Moral 'Scepticism'" *Philosophy* **57** (1982): 173-191.

[22] Mackie, *Ethics*, pp. 36-42.

action is a deliberate piece of cruelty. The wrongness of such an action must somehow be dependent on this fact: the action is wrong *because* it is a piece of deliberate cruelty. But what can "because" signify here? The relation must somehow be a necessary one; yet how are we to make sense of this necessity? The epistemological correlate of all this is that to be aware of such ontologically peculiar entities we would have to posit some special faculty of moral intuition distinct from our ordinary epistemic faculties.

These arguments, however, are uncompelling.[23] The argument from relativity can be rebutted on several grounds. In the first place it is by no means clear that the degree of variation between moral codes is as great as Mackie makes out. Presumably at the core of morality are the rules that make human society possible.[24] It is hard, for instance, to conceive of something that would count as a moral code which did not try to curtail those forms of anti-social behaviour (such as wanton and random killing of one's fellows) that would render the existence of society impossible. It may be, then, that there is a core morality common to all moral codes; certainly the empirical evidence is not decisively against such an hypothesis. In fact, Mackie does consider such a possibility. However he then argues that even if there is little or no variation in moral *principles*, morality is not exhausted by principles or codes. Moral *ideals* do exhibit the relevant sort of variation and hence count against the objectivity of values. But this argument, even if it goes through, will not show that there are no objective moral values; only that there are no objective moral ideals. Moreover, Mackie's only proffered reason for holding that there are no objective moral ideals is that there frequently arises disagreement about the value of particular things because they exhibit some property which arouses certain responses immediately in some people, though different responses in others. Even if this disagreement exists, it does nothing to impugn objectivism about whether the things in question have the property in dispute or not. The property which arouses the response may in fact be the objective value of the object; that people can misapprehend this quality does not show that it is not objectively there.

---

[23] What follows here is indebted to the much fuller criticisms presented in Michael Wreen, "Mackie on the Objectivity of Values" *Dialectica* **39** (1985): 147-156.

[24] Cf. P. F. Strawson, "Social Morality and Individual Ideal" *Philosophy* **36** (1961): 1-17.

Nor is the argument from queerness any more convincing. First, the objectivist does not hold that values are "intrinsically prescriptive" if by that it is meant that an objective good would necessarily be sought by anyone acquainted with it. Objectivist theories of value can consistently allow, for example, that an agent may both recognize the objective value of an action and still (perhaps due to weakness of will, or just plain wickedness) fail to perform that action. Second, the question of the supposedly queer relation between an object's valuational properties and its natural properties can only arise in the form Mackie proposes if it is assumed that the objectivist is committed to the thesis that value is a non-natural property. Many objectivists have, of course, been naturalists about value (e.g. Aristotle, Bentham, Mill, Sidgwick). Third, even if the objectivist is a non-naturalist about value he may very well see no particularly embarrassing queerness in the relation between an object's non-natural valuational properties and its natural properties. Hence goodness, for instance, might be held to be an emergent quality causally related to its grounding properties. The "because" the necessity of which worries Mackie is thus some sort of causal "because" and has the same sort of necessity that causal relations are often claimed to have (i.e. weaker than logical necessity, stronger than mere contingency). Difficulties in specifying precisely what this causal necessity is are not, then, special to a non-naturalist theory of value; many familiar theories of causation face the same problem.[25] Alternatively, the non-naturalist may decide to utilize the notion of supervenience to explain the relation of an object's valuational properties to its natural properties; a notion increasingly invoked in other areas of philosophy than the theory of value, whatever the difficulties of giving a precise explication of it are.

The epistemological correlate of the argument from ontological queerness is also uncompelling. Obviously the objectivist who is a naturalist is not going to need to posit any special intuitive faculty to perceive values. But neither need the non-naturalist commit himself to the existence of such a faculty. He may very well just say that valuational reasoning is on a par with ordinary everyday reasoning. To the objection that a valuational conclusion can only be inferred from a valuational premise, he may reply

---

[25] To be fair Mackie would presumably reply to this by saying that elsewhere he has elaborated a theory of causation free from this defect: see his *The Cement of the Universe: A Study of Causation* (Oxford: Clarendon Press, 1974).

ad hominem that similar problems face the justification of inductive or deductive reasoning (which the critic presumably accepts as legitimate). Whatever solution is adequate to vindicate the objectivity of the latter will presumably also serve for the former. Thus either (i) all objects, properties and relations are subjective (and hence values are not any queerer than any other entity); or (ii) valuational properties are objective.

V

I conclude, then, that Mackie has failed to establish his case against the objective existence of values. Of course, to discredit some arguments against the thesis that there are objective values is not equivalent to establishing the truth of that thesis. Nor do I intend here and now to try to present any positive arguments for the thesis, though it is perhaps worth mentioning that as far as Mackie himself is concerned our ordinary evaluative language is so shot through with ontological commitment to the objectivity of values that the burden of proof must rest with the subjectivist. I do, however, want to say something about a possible objection which might be raised against me at this point. I have argued so far that we might justify the adoption of a philosophical theory that deliberately suppressed certain of our intuitions (as, for example, those about the subjective) on the grounds that the theory need only capture those intuitions relevant for a particular purpose. I have further pointed out that such a metaphilosophical view can escape the charge of complete relativism by embracing a belief in an ultimate objective value. I have then tried to show that there is no reason to deny the existence of objective values (and hence presumably also no reason to deny that there might be an ultimate objective value). But now it may be objected that all I have done is just to reintroduce intuitions through the back door. Intuitions about value are now presumably basic and occupy the office of those fundamental low-level intuitions that, according to the modified intuitive realist view mentioned earlier, regulate philosophical theorizing.

There is some justice in such a charge, particularly if it is claimed that objective valuational properties are non-natural properties. For such a thesis has often gone together with a belief in a special faculty of moral intuition. (Hence non-naturalism is sometimes referred to as intuitionism, even though the non-naturalist is by no means committed to asserting the existence of such a special faculty.) However, as we have noted several times now, objectivism is also compatible with naturalism about values. Moreover there is an important difficulty with non-naturalism: the supervenience problem.[26] Non-naturalism has to admit the possibility of two objects having exactly similar natural properties but dissimilar valuational properties. Thus, for example, two actions or two paintings might be exactly similar in respect of all their natural properties and yet one action be right and the other wrong, one painting beautiful and the other ugly. Now the non-naturalist certainly denies that an object's possession of any natural property can *entail* its possession of a non-natural valuational property. However, he surely wants to admit that there is some sort of dependence relation between an object's natural and non-natural properties; an object is valuable somehow *because* it has certain natural properties. But if an action is right somehow *because* of its natural features, or a painting beautiful *because* of its natural features, then it seems implausible to maintain that two such objects could agree in their natural properties and yet differ in their valuational properties. The non-naturalist's reply must be to appeal to the existence of a necessary but non-analytic connection, with the attendant difficulties of such a claim.

Is naturalism any more satisfactory though? In the first place it is important to note that naturalism about values can take at least two forms. The more familiar form is one which maintains that possession of a valuational property just is possession of a natural property (e.g. "good" just means "conducive to the greatest happiness in the greatest number"). But the naturalist might instead hold a slightly different thesis: viz. that though valuational properties are distinct from natural properties, possession of the former is entailed by possession of certain of the latter.[27] (Compare the way "He owns eleven cars" entails "The number of cars he owns is equal to the next prime

---

[26] Cf. R. M. Hare, *The Language of Morals* (Oxford: Clarendon Press, 1952), pp. 80-81.

[27] For a defence of this sort of naturalism see R. G. Swinburne, "The Objectivity of Morality" *Philosophy* **51** (1976): 5-20.

number greater than seven", even though the latter says something very different from the former.)

Now it is sometimes thought that naturalism has long ago been refuted by G. E. Moore in his *Principia Ethica* (sect. 13). Moore utilizes what is sometimes called an "open question argument" to show that "good" is indefinable in terms of any natural property. The argument goes: If "good" was definable as "possessing P" (where P is some natural property), then it ought to make no sense to ask "Is the possession of P a good thing?" However, it always does make sense to ask this. Consider, for example, naturalistic candidates for defining "good" like "conducive to the happiness of the greatest number" or "in accord with the will of God". Clearly it is sensible to ask, "Is an action conducive to the greatest happiness of the greatest number a good action?" or "Is obedience to God's will a good thing?" Hence "good" cannot mean the same as "possessing P" where P is a natural property.

However this argument is inconclusive, especially if (as Moore thought) it is supposed to show not only that "good" is indefinable, but that it denotes a unique property not denoted by any other expression. Consider the expressions "white" and "the colour of fresh snow". These differ in meaning (sense) but presumably designate the same property. Hence from the fact that the question "Is the colour of fresh snow white?" is meaningful, it does not follow that these two non-synonymous expressions do not denote the same property. Similarly, it may very well still be true that the property of goodness is identical with some natural property P, even if (i) "good" does not mean the same as "possessing P", and (ii) the question "Is the possession of P a good thing?" is always meaningful.[28]

Nor is a well known argument of Hare's any more convincing.[29] Hare argues that if it were true that "a good A" meant the same as "an A which is C" (where "C" is a descriptive term) then it would be impossible to use the sentence "An A which is C is good" to commend A's which are C. This is because the sentence would then be analytic and equivalent to "An A which is C is C". But we do use such sentences to

---

[28] Cf. R. G. Durrant, "Identity of Properties and the Definition of 'Good'" *Australasian Journal of Philosophy* **48** (1970): 360-361 which also points out that Moore's own referential theory of meaning blinded him to this possibility.

[29] Hare, pp. 90-91.

commend, hence naturalism is refuted. However, in the first place, the fact that value judgements are often used to commend does not show that they do not ascribe natural properties. One may commend by using sentences like "He is an extremely hard working person", "This is real silk", "She will become very famous".[30] Moreover, once again the second type of naturalism would be unaffected by such an objection since it does not assert that "good" *means* "C" (where "C" is some descriptive term).

Of course, these brief remarks are not offered as a full-scale defence of a naturalistic account of value. For the moment all I'm concerned to do here is sketch out a prima facie feasible position about value which, if sound, could justify my earlier metaphilosophical suggestion. That is, my suggestion that it is possible to have a metaphilosophy which is not entirely relativistic and yet which nevertheless assesses the adequacy of philosophical theories in terms of their relevance to particular purposes. Provided value is objective, this need not collapse into complete relativism (especially if there is an ultimate objective value). Moreover, if value is naturalistic then intuitions need not play an important role in the system at all. Hence it might well be that however deep-rooted our intuitions about the subjective are, we nevertheless (*pace* Nagel) ought to be doing our best to get rid of them. (Perhaps, for example, they foster a sense of egoistic concern which is not conducive to an higher objective good.) Anyway, even if it is true that there is a subjective viewpoint on my own death which cannot be captured in a purely objective viewpoint, it remains to be shown that this is something I ought to be worried about trying to capture in my philosophical theorizing.

---

[30] Cf. Swinburne, p. 9n

CHAPTER 3: THE FEAR OF DEATH

I

Is it reasonable to fear death? In this chapter I want to consider two ancient Epicurean arguments to the conclusion that it is not. The first maintains that death cannot be an evil for a dead person because that "evil" could have no subject. The second maintains that to fear the prospect of one's future nonexistence is unreasonable because no one feels it reasonable to find it distressing to contemplate the eternity before his or her coming into existence. In the course of attempting to disarm these two arguments I shall present a positive argument for the reasonableness of fearing death (though I shall note that this argument does not entail that a desire for immortality is also reasonable). Finally I shall conclude with some remarks about the way in which a reasonable fear of death can easily become an unreasonable one and suggest that a concern with this possibility has motivated quite dissimilar positions on this question.

II

Clearly the rationality of fearing death is closely tied to one's beliefs about the prospect of post-mortem survival. Thus if I believe that I shall survive death, then my fear of death may very well be dependent upon my beliefs about what may befall me after death. Suppose, for example, I subscribe to a traditional picture that dominated Western culture for centuries whereby death is understood to be an event which precedes divine judgement and subsequent punishment or reward. Given such an eschatology, it is presumably rational for me to fear death on the grounds that I am anxious about the post-mortem fate which will immediately befall me. (Though it is conceded that here it is not death qua death that I fear; death is the indirect object of my fear rather than the direct object.) Of course, the rationality of a fear of death based on the belief in judgement and eternal damnation rests partly on the rationality of that belief. If the belief is strongly rational then it is certainly rational to fear death. However, if the belief is not irrational, i.e. it is a belief that is by no means proved but is not substantially inferior epistemically to its rivals, then it is also rational to fear death. Furthermore, if there is even a small, non-negligible probability of post-mortem judgement and eternal damnation then, depending on how great a disvalue Hell is, it is still rational to fear death. In other words, the belief in survival and subsequent damnation has to be strongly irrational, of zero probability, in order to rule out the rationality of a fear of death based upon anxiety about the possibility of a post-mortem judgement. And this is surely a very strong premise to have to grant.

However, what if we do refuse to concede the rationality of any such beliefs about the reality of an afterlife? What if we believe it to be an empirical certainty that death coincides with the permanent destruction of the sentient subject? Many who believe this to be so nevertheless fear death. Is such a fear unreasonable? The classical Epicurean tradition certainly thought so and presented two important arguments to this effect.

The first of our two ancient arguments is put by Epicurus thus:

> So death, the most terrifying of ills, is nothing to us, since so long as we exist, death is not with us; but when death comes, then we do not exist. It does not then concern either the living or the dead, since for the former it is not, and the latter are no more (*Letter to Menoeceus*, 125).[1]

Obviously this argument needs a few qualifications to get going. First and question-beggingly, that death coincides with permanent extinction. Second, that it is the state of death rather than the process of dying that is no evil. Third, that it is only whether death is an evil for the person who dies that is being considered, not whether the person's death is an evil for others. But notwithstanding these extra assumptions (which we will grant throughout) many philosophers have been unwilling to accept the Epicurean argument.

---

[1] *Epicurus: The Extant Remains*, trans. Cyril Bailey (Oxford: Clarendon Press, 1926), p. 85.

Now in its original context the Epicurean argument involves the conviction that all good and evil consists in sensation. Hence because when dead we experience no pain, death cannot be an evil. The argument thus understood would minimally have made the point that, given death is equivalent to the annihilation of the sentient subject, the fear of death cannot be reasonably identified with the fear of an unpleasant future *experience*. However the argument has a more general formulation that can be removed from the original hedonistic framework. This consists in arguing that death cannot be an evil for the dead person because, *ex hypothesi*, there is no longer any subject for such an evil. Hence we ought not to fear death.

Most writers have conceded Epicurus' point that something cannot be an evil for the dead person and have sought to locate the evil of death elsewhere: e.g. by claiming that death is a "negative" evil consisting in the privation or loss of the goods of life. Since life is a precondition for the enjoyment of these other goods, it is reasonable to regard death as an evil to be avoided.[2] But the Epicurean is unsatisfied by this reply. Just as life is a precondition for these other goods, so too is it a precondition for other evils. That I am alive, argues the Epicurean, is a presupposition of any claim that something is a good or evil for me and thus death cannot coherently be said to be either a good or an evil for me. It is not just that when dead I will not be conscious of the evil that has befallen me, but rather that once dead there ceases to be a subject to be affected for good or evil.[3]

Epicurus' argument maintains, then, that it is incoherent to claim that death is an evil for the dead person because the subject of the supposed evil no longer exists. I want to challenge this claim by defending the paradoxical notion that something could coherently be said to be an evil for a dead person, i.e. that the dead can be harmed.

---

[2] This position is defended in Bernard Williams, *Problems of the Self* (Cambridge: Cambridge University Press, 1973), Ch. 6; and in Thomas Nagel, *Mortal Questions*, Ch. 1.

[3] This feature of the Epicurean argument is duly stressed in Harry S. Silverstein, "The Evil of Death" *Journal of Philosophy* 77 (1980): 401-424. Silverstein's counter, however, is unsatisfactory. He suggests that my death coexists timelessly with me and is thus a possible object of my suffering. But Epicurus' point is that because I won't be there to be affected by my death when it occurs, my death cannot be reasonably viewed as the occasion of loss to me in the same way as my wife's death yesterday can be—notwithstanding the fact that both deaths coexist atemporally.

III

The notion that a dead person can be harmed is not a new one. In the *Nicomachean Ethics* (I, 10) Aristotle speaks of it thus:

A dead person is popularly believed to be capable of experiencing both good and ill fortune — honour and dishonour, and prosperity and the loss of it among his children and descendants generally — in exactly the same way as if he were alive but unaware or unobservant of what was happening.[4]

More recently Joel Feinberg has argued that, even given that death is the total and final end of the person, dead persons may be harmed after their deaths for they may still have their interests invaded posthumously by actions like the abrogation of their wills, reneging on contracts, breaking promises and the maligning of their reputations.[5] Feinberg presents three basic arguments for this conception of posthumous interest.

The first of these turns upon a distinction (first proposed by W. D. Ross) between the *fulfilment* of a want and the *satisfaction* of a want. Fulfilment requires merely that what is wanted comes into existence; whereas satisfaction requires the pleasant feeling of contentment or gratification that normally occurs in the mind of the desirer when she believes that her desire has been fulfilled. Harm to an interest is then explicated in terms of non-fulfilment of a want rather than non-satisfaction of a want. If interests are fulfilled only by what is desired coming into existence, then there can survive posthumous interests that can be fulfilled only by the coming into existence of what is desired. Feinberg proposes that we think of all harm as done to interests themselves, and interpret talk of harm done to men and women as convenient elliptical references to, and identification of, the interest that was thwarted or set back.

The second argument maintains that because the objects of a person's interests are usually wanted or aimed at events that occur outside of her immediate experience and

---

[4] Aristotle, *Ethics*, trans. J. A. K. Thomson (Harmondsworth: Penguin Books, 1953), p. 45.

[5] Feinberg originally proposed this view in papers reprinted in his *Rights, Justice and the Bounds of Liberty* (Princeton: Princeton University Press, 1980), especially pp. 59-68, 173-176. More recently, however, he has modified his position somewhat: see his *Harm to Others* (New York: Oxford University Press, 1984), Ch. 2.

at some future time, the area of a person's good or harm is necessarily wider than her subjective experience and longer than her biological life. For example, a person's interest in maintaining a good reputation after his death is an interest that can survive that person's death. It is one of a kind of interest that is responsive to a person's desires to stand in certain relations to other people.

The third argument replies to the obvious objection: How can a dead person be harmed by what she cannot be aware of? Feinberg argues that a person can be harmed though not affected by the harm. In other words, what I don't know *can* harm me. For example, if someone libels me and I never learn of this libel, I have nevertheless been injured in virtue of the harm done my interest in a good reputation. But if knowledge isn't a necessary condition of harm before my death, why is it necessary afterwards? Thus the dead (like the living) can be harmed without being aware of it, even though (also like the living) they cannot be embarrassed or distressed at that of which they are unaware.

IV

Feinberg's account has been criticized on various grounds.[6] Common to these objections is the conviction that it is senseless to suppose there can be interests without an interest-bearer. Thus it is argued: (a) the claim that a person has an interest in a posthumous event can only remain true so long as that interest has a bearer, i.e. so long as the person is alive; and (b) since Feinberg admits that interests are "stakes" that are derived from and linked to wants, then a dead person by ceasing to have wants ceases to have interests. And indeed Feinberg himself now believes that his earlier account of posthumous harm is unsatisfactory because the surviving interests must be the interests of someone or other.[7] He claims that they cannot be the interests of the

---

[6] See André Gombay, "What You Don't Know Doesn't Hurt You" *Proceedings of the Aristotelian Society* 79 (1978-79): 239-249; Ernest Partridge, "Posthumous Interest and Posthumous Respect" *Ethics* 91 (1981): 243-264; Barbara Baum Levenbook, "Harming Someone After His Death" *Ethics* 94 (1984): 407-419; Don Marquis, "Harming the Dead" *Ethics* 96 (1985): 159-161; and Barbara Baum Levenbook, "Harming the Dead, Once Again" *Ethics* 96 (1985): 162-164.

[7] Cf. Feinberg, *Harm to Others*, pp. 89-91.

dead person who no longer exists since he or she cannot now have any want-based interests. Nor can the detached interests themselves be the proper subject of harm for they are either nobody's interests at all and hence not morally considerable, or they are the interests of some Absolute Mind — a gratuitous metaphysical assumption. His solution to this difficulty is to retain the concept of posthumous harm and maintain that it is the interests of the living person who is no longer with us which are harmed by events at or after that person's death. To do this he takes over a distinction of George Pitcher's between (i) a description of an ante-mortem person after his death, and (ii) a description of a post-mortem person after his death.[8] It is then conceded that post-mortem persons cannot be harmed. However an ante-mortem person can be harmed by an unfortunate event after his death in the sense that the occurrence of the event makes it true that during the time before the person's death he was harmed — harmed in that the unfortunate event was going to happen.

That we have moral intuitions to the effect that certain actions can somehow harm the dead seems indubitable. This is perhaps clearer if we leave off arguing about promises to the dead to consider instead three macabre cases where there seems to be a strong feeling present that some wrong has been done the dead. Firstly then, imagine that I break into a tomb and take away a skull to use as a paperweight on my desk. I might be condemned for this action on various grounds: trespassing on private property, causing the dead man's relatives distress (if he has any, of course) and so on. But surely one ground that might be invoked is the idea that what I have done is somehow a harm to the dead man, that I have offered an indignity to the dead as someone might want to say. Again, by way of a second example consider the phenomenon of body-snatching. The illicit exhuming of corpses for dissection was (and is) condemned not merely on grounds of distress to relatives etc. but also once again because of the widespread feeling that such a practice is an affront to the dead person.

Now someone might be unimpressed by these examples. While conceding that some people will feel that such practices are an affront to the dead, such an interlocuter might reply that all this is mere superstition. Such plausibility as it has is

---

[8] See George Pitcher, "The Misfortunes of the Dead" *American Philosophical Quarterly* 21 (1984): 183-188.

due only to an illegitimate trading on the concealed picture of a dead person as somehow involving a sentient remainder. Moreover he might point out that our Western
concern with the privacy of tombs and not disturbing the bodies of the dead is,
historically speaking, quite a recent phenomenon dating only from the eighteenth
century.[9] In other words, the prima facie "naturalness" of our current attitudes
towards the dead will not survive historical and analytical investigation.

I am unconvinced that this sort of reply does justice to these examples but I'll
waive that at present because it does seem clear that such a proposed reply is
insufficient to deal with my third example: the case of (non-consenting) necrophilia.
Surely our moral distaste for such acts of necrophilia involves more than just the con-
demnation of a sexual perversion. Part of what is morally distasteful is the element of
violation of a dead person, of posthumous rape. (And, of course, it would be possible
to imagine cases where this element was precisely the intent of the necrophiliac.) If
this is so then who is being harmed by this rape, who is being violated, but the dead
person? And this feeling need not rest upon any belief (superstitious or otherwise) in
the possibility of a sentient remainder of the dead person being present during the act.
Feinberg's account has at least the advantage of enabling us to justify coherently this
sense of a harm done to the dead person in terms of a posthumous invasion of his
interests.

Of course, there are metaphysical costs still to be counted if we opt for such a
position. In the first place the espousal of a theory of posthumous harms which
recognizes a harm to a person when the act that does the harm post-dates her might
very well seem to commit us to the existence of some variety of backward causation.
Pitcher and Feinberg, however, both deny such an implication. The occurrence of the
posthumous harm does not entail backward causation because physical causation is not
involved here. Rather the occurrence of the harmful posthumous event *makes it true*
that the ante-mortem person was harmed, it is *responsible* for the ante-mortem harm.
To illuminate the senses of "make true" and "responsible for" involved here Pitcher
offers an analogy:

---

[9] Cf. the historical discussion in Phillipe Ariès, *Western Attitudes Toward Death: From the Middle
Ages to the Present* (Baltimore: John Hopkins University Press, 1974).

If the world should be blasted to smithereens during the next presidency after Ronald Reagan's, this would make it true (be responsible for the fact) that even now, during Reagan's term, he is the penultimate president of the United States.[10]

Pitcher and Feinberg hasten to add this does not mean that on the occurrence of the posthumous event it suddenly *becomes* true that the ante-mortem person was harmed; rather it becomes apparent to us for the first time that it was true all along.

Now there may be difficulties with all this, but for the moment what I want to point out it that this account is by no means metaphysically neutral. It apparently commits us, for example, to some sort of realism about the future — for otherwise how can future states of affairs make it true *now* that I will be harmed after my death? Anti-realist philosophers, however, often deny that statements about the future have present truth-values. The Pitcher-Feinberg account just begs this whole question. Indeed given that the Pitcher-Feinberg account is metaphysically freighted in this way it seems worth briefly sketching out a different sort of account of posthumous harm; one that admittedly does involve certain metaphysical commitments, but arguably no more so than the Pitcher-Feinberg view.

The alternative account I have in mind admits posthumous harm but denies that the subject of harm is the ante-mortem person; rather the subject of harm is (as Feinberg originally suggested) the dead person's *interests*. The first objection to this proposal was that interests require an interest-bearer; the second objection was that since interests are linked to wants, a dead person by ceasing to have wants ceases to have interests. In fact neither objection is overwhelming.

Firstly, even if an interest requires a bearer (i.e. a logical subject) it doesn't follow that the bearer must be alive. Perhaps all that interests require are *logical subjects*. It is important to distinguish between death (conceived of here as involving permanent lack of consciousness, experiencelessness) and lack of a logical subject. It is arguable that a particular (e.g. David Hume) does not cease to be a particular after his death. He still has properties (e.g. having been a philosopher) and, given the argument is sound, interests are among these properties. Nor is this as odd as all that for, while death may

---

[10] Pitcher, p. 188.

involve experiencelessness, experiencelessness doesn't entail lack of interests. Thus a comatose person is apparently in a state of consciouslessness or experiencelessness without it entailing that such a person has no interests.[11] Secondly, the link between wants and interests doesn't necessarily mean that a dead person by ceasing to have wants ceases to have interests. Interests may be linked to wants without "X has no wants (now)" entailing "X has no interests (now)". Consider once again the case of the comatose patient.

The account I am proposing here, then, allows that persons can have interests provided that they have had desires and aims, even if they no longer have them. This permits us to ascribe interests to the comatose, as well as to the dead. At first sight this might seem a little counterintuitive, but surely it only represents the mirror image of a more familiar claim: viz. that future persons have interests even though they do not presently have desires and aims, provided that they will (or would) have them. Much current writing in environmental ethics, for example, assumes that future beings (beings who do not now exist) nevertheless have interests which can be presently invaded. If it is conceded that we can now harm the interests of future generations by polluting the environment or exhausting non-renewable resources, then the present possession of desires and aims cannot be a necessary condition of having interests. And if it is not, then it seems plausible to suppose that there is no special difficulty in holding that the dead have interests that can be posthumously harmed.

Thus on either the Pitcher-Feinberg account or on the alternative account I have just sketched it makes sense to talk of harm done to the dead in terms of posthumous invasion of their interests. This in turn allows us to say that evil can indeed befall the dead; from which it follows that Epicurus' argument for the unreasonableness of fearing death is unsound.

---

[11] In *Rights, Justice and the Bounds of Liberty* (p. 177) in a discussion of "human vegetables" Feinberg denies this, claiming that capacities to have certain experiences at a particular time are necessary in order to have interests at that time. In *Harm to Others* he revises this view and abandons the claim that capacities are necessary conditions of interests.

V

Not only does our discussion so far dispose of the first Epicurean argument against fearing death, it also provides the basis for an argument for the reasonableness of fearing death. Firstly, recall again the distinction between the satisfaction of a desire and its fulfilment. Obviously one does not entail the other. Thus the fulfilment of my desire may bring me satisfaction but also quite commonly it does not. Similarly I can experience satisfaction of a desire without fulfilment if I falsely believe that the desire has been fulfilled. Moreover it also seems that satisfaction could occur before the desirer believes that her desire has been fulfilled, so long as she is reasonably certain it will be fulfilled. This is important because it means dissatisfaction may correspondingly take place *before* the agent believes the desire has not been fulfilled, i.e. when she is certain or reasonably certain that the desire will not be fulfilled.

Secondly, note that not every desire creates an interest. For example, I may desire that a particular horse win the Melbourne Cup but, unless I own the horse or have a bet riding on the race, it would be odd to say that I have an interest in that horse winning the Cup. I have to have some "stake" arising out of my desire for an interest to result.

Now if an agent has any interest that death will thwart then death is a potential harm to that agent. But since (i) most desires are future-directed and (ii) death may come at any time, then a desire the fulfilment of which requires one's being alive may create an interest which makes the fear of death reasonable. Death threatens its non-fulfilment. Moreover the reasonable expectation of such non-fulfilment can also cause present dissatisfaction. Of course it may be argued that some desires are such that it is unreasonable to have them, but the Epicurean has to argue that it is unreasonable to have *any* desire which may create an interest the fulfilment of which requires one's being alive: e.g. my desire to complete this chapter. And this is surely too much for us to grant.

Nevertheless this argument does need some qualification. In the first place while it thus seems reasonable to wish to postpone our deaths if our interests will be thwarted by our dying, it doesn't thereby follow that a desire for immortality is a reasonable one. For example, there may be grounds for holding that the desire to live forever will generate an interest that is bound to lead to dissatisfaction and lack of fulfilment if there is reasonable certainty that such a state of affairs will not obtain. In this sense it could be argued that such a desire is unreasonable. Secondly, some desires are such that immortality would be a necessary condition of their fulfilment though the desire itself is a trivial one. For example, suppose I conceive a desire that I should begin to recite the series of positive integers and for every integer I recite thereafter recite its successor. Since the series is an infinite one, the fulfilment of this desire will require my infinitely continued existence. Yet such a desire hardly qualifies as a reasonable ground for my desiring to be immortal. In other words, though I have presented a positive argument for the reasonableness of fearing death under certain conditions I don't believe that this argument entails the reasonableness of a desire for immortality.

Finally, it is important to note that an interest can clash with present desires. For example, I have an interest in my continued good health that can clash with my present desire not to take the bitter-tasting quinine tablets in a malarial zone. My interest in my continued good health should reasonably override this present desire because my continued good health is generally a precondition of the harmonious advancement of all my other interests. This point enables us to deal with a special case like the following. Imagine a prisoner whose life has become unbearable. Every day he is taken from his cell and tortured. There is no hope of release from this condition and his captors have eliminated any possibility of his taking his own life. He desires nothing so much as to die. However, given the impossibility of achieving this he sets himself day to day goals to help alleviate the rigours of his existence. Let's suppose he is an architect and every day he constructs a building in his imagination. His desire to finish constructing his imaginary buildings is, of course, one that death will thwart if it comes. Nevertheless, given that his desire to die has created an overriding interest in his own death, it seems that this interest should reasonably override any desire to complete his buildings should the possibility of a clash between them arise. Although death would thwart his desire to complete his buildings it would not harm his interests.

VI

The second Epicurean argument for the unreasonableness of fearing death was presented by Lucretius, Epicurus' disciple. He pointed out that to fear the prospect of one's nonexistence after death is odd when we consider that the supposition of our nonexistence before birth (or conception) generally causes no corresponding distress (*De Rerum Natura*, III, 973-7). That this argument has had some actual persuasive force is suggested by Boswell's report of his interview with the dying David Hume:

> I asked him if the thought of Annihilation never gave him any uneasiness. He said not the least; no more than the thought that he had not been, as Lucretius observes.[12]

Thomas Nagel, while conceding that most people do not view their future non-existence in the same way as their past nonexistence, argues that this is not surprising. Death is not "simply the mirror image of the prior abyss" and hence it is reasonable to regard them differently. The time after a person's death is time in which, if he had not died, he would be alive. In other words, it is time of which the person has been deprived by his death.

> But we cannot say that the time prior to a man's birth is time in which he would have lived had he been born not then but earlier. For aside from the brief margin permitted by premature labor, he *could* not have been born earlier: anyone born substantially earlier than he was would have been someone else. Therefore the time prior to his birth is not time in which his subsequent birth prevents him from living. His birth, when it occurs, does not entail the loss to him of any life whatever.[13]

In a footnote Nagel confesses to "being troubled by the above argument, on the ground that it is too sophisticated to explain the simple difference between our

---

[12] "An Account of My Last Interview with David Hume, Esq." in David Hume, *Dialogues Concerning Natural Religion*, ed. Norman Kemp Smith (Indianapolis: Bobbs-Merrill, 1962), p. 77.

[13] Nagel, *Mortal Questions*, p. 8.

attitudes to prenatal and posthumous existence." He then recounts a science fiction scenario to suggest that "something about the future *prospect* of permanent nothingness is not captured by the analysis in terms of denied possibilities." However Nagel's argument has other difficulties to it than the one he mentions.[14] In the first place note that the argument has far reaching consequences. For example, if time is absolute then it would make sense to suppose that all the events that take place took place earlier (by any amount). But if Nagel is right some events couldn't have taken place earlier (births, or perhaps it would be better for him to single out conceptions). Hence his view must be incompatible with absolute time. While, of course, absolute time may indeed be an erroneous conception, the attendant rejection of the theory by Nagel's argument seems a very *large* consequence to follow from such a small point.

But, whatever the correct view of time may be, Nagel's argument suffers from a more fundamental implausibility since on his account I could not have been born before I was and still be *me*. That is, the time of a person's birth is an *essential* property of that person. Although detectable only empirically, it is nonetheless a metaphysically necessary property in that anyone lacking that property could not be that person. Thus Nagel is committed to asserting that the proposition that David Hume was born on 26 April 1711 if true is necessarily true, yet what the proposition says cannot be known a priori. This position has some odd consequences.[15]

By making the time of a person's birth an essential property in this way it follows that I cannot be certain that the person before me really is David Hume unless it is true that he was born on 26 April 1711. The epistemological situation that I am in examining David Hume is compatible with it being someone else (Boswell perhaps) that I am examining. Until the matter of the time of birth is settled I cannot be sure that

---

[14] In his *Reasons and Persons* (Oxford: Clarendon Press, 1984), p. 175 Derek Parfit suggests that this sort of argument is unsatisfactory because even if it is logically impossible that we might have been born earlier, it is nevertheless possible to regret truths even when it is logically impossible that these truths be false. Hence, for example, the Pythagoreans regretted that the square root of two was not a rational number when they learnt this. This objection, however, is irrelevant. The Epicurean point is that it is not *reasonable* to regret one's prenatal nonexistence, not that it is not *possible* to do so. Nagel's argument then tries to show *why* it is irrational to regret one's past nonexistence; it doesn't claim that one *cannot* regret this.

[15] My argument here is indebted to Pavel Tichý's criticisms of a similar notion of Kripke's in "Kripke on Necessity A Posteriori" *Philosophical Studies* 43 (1983): 232-241.

it is David Hume I am dealing with. However, in order to establish that the person before me has the essential property of being born on 26 April 1711 I have to inspect that person. But unless I already know that the person has that essential property I cannot be sure that I am inspecting the right person.

How can we evade this peculiar epistemic circle? One possibility is to claim that essential properties can be known a priori. But, given that a person's time of birth is taken to be an essential property, it seems highly implausible to maintain that I can be sure that David Hume was born on 26 April 1711 prior to any empirical investigation. A more promising move is to admit that numerical identity of objects is unproblematic epistemically. But this involves abandoning individual essentialism and with it Nagel's reply to Lucretius.

VII

That there is an asymmetry between our attitudes to prenatal and posthumous nonexistence seems to be true enough. One way to try to account for a feeling that a desire for prenatal existence is somehow unreasonable might be to point out that being born earlier wouldn't satisfy someone who is distressed by her previous infinite non-existence. No matter how much earlier she came into existence there would always remain an infinite amount of previous time. Thus someone who regrets the loss of prenatal existence is really regretting the fact that she has not always existed throughout the infinite past. Perhaps it is this that seems unreasonable. But, on the other hand, it is the lack of infinite future existence that is feared in the case of death and the desire for infinite future existence is not generally considered an unreasonable one. Is it somehow more reasonable to desire to be a being with a beginning but no end rather than to be an eternal being (i.e. a being with neither beginning nor end)?

Interestingly Aquinas represents the condition of being a being with a beginning but no end as the actual state of angels and human souls. They have a beginning by divine creation but having been created they continue to exist forever (unless God should will their destruction). Thomists sometimes therefore refer to such beings as intrinsically but not extrinsically necessary beings. God, however, is both intrinsically and extrinsically necessary. God is uncreated and has no beginning or end in time. He, in this special sense, exists *eternally*. Thus the desire to exist eternally (rather than the desire never to die) should perhaps be seen by the Thomist not merely as unreasonable but rather as positively *blasphemous*, for it requires that one be God, or at least God qua uncreated necessary being. For a theist this might be a possible explanation for the asymmetry under consideration.

But be that as it may, note also that the asymmetry in our attitudes to past non-existence and future nonexistence is reflected in the asymmetry of our attitudes to the condition of being what I shall call a "past-sempiternal being" (i.e. a being with no beginning but an end) or a "future-sempiternal being" (i.e. a being with a beginning but no end). Past-sempiternals have something to fear whereas future-sempiternals do not. Future-sempiternals may have some regrets about their past nonexistence whereas past-sempiternals cannot. Now given a choice between being past- or future-sempiternal then, (provided the quality of life is good in both cases), surely we would opt for being future-sempiternal. For one thing, at any moment a past-sempiternal only ever has a finite amount of time left. Now, of course, the mirror image of this is that at any moment a past-sempiternal has had an infinite amount of experience while the future-sempiternal has at any moment only had a finite amount. The reason why this mirror condition is nevertheless not so distressing for the future-sempiternal and not so comforting for the past-sempiternal is the basic asymmetry of our attitudes to past and future pains and pleasures. Past ones don't really matter as much to us as future ones. Indeed this is highlighted if we retract our earlier condition that the quality of experience in both the past- and future-sempiternal cases is equally *good* and stipulate instead that it be equally *horrendous*. In that case we surely would opt to be past-sempiternals with only a finite period of time left to endure rather than future-sempiternals with an infinity of pain to look forward to.

This asymmetry of our attitudes to past and future pain is strikingly revealed in the following fantasy of Robert Nozick's:

> Suppose you have gone into hospital for a very painful operation. No anesthetic can be given for this operation, though something can be given immediately afterwards causing you to forget the trauma. This puts you to sleep, and when you awake you will not remember what happened. Each

night of the preliminary stay in the hospital, you are given a sedative to induce sleep; each morning you wake up and wonder whether the tremendously painful operation has happened already or is still to come. Are you indifferent as to which it is, counting pain in your life as the same whenever it happens? No, you hope it has happened already and is behind you. If the nurse comes in and tells you the operation is over, you are relieved; if she says that today is the day, you are fearful. Although in any case it is three hours of agonizing pain that you undergo, you want it to be over and done.[16]

Nozick goes on to make a further claim that this asymmetry between future and past in the first-person case disappears when we consider a third-person case for "if another person is in this situation, with no danger involved, only pain, it does not matter to you whether he had it yesterday or will have it tomorrow."[17] This is surely false. If a loved one is in this hospital situation then when I think of her I naturally wish for her that the operation is over. On the other hand, if an enemy of mine is in that situation and I catch myself wishing that his operation be still to come, then I naturally find this wish malicious and morally reprehensible. In other words, this asymmetry is by no means limited to first-person cases but rather is a basic feature of our attitudes to past and future pains and pleasures. Our attitudes to past and future nonexistence in turn reflect these former attitudes. Whether they can be called reasonable or not is not entirely clear. They certainly don't seem *unreasonable*, though it may be that they should be viewed as non-rational altogether.[18] However the phenomenon of this asymmetry of attitudes supports at least a minimal argument against Lucretius to the effect that our asymmetrical attitudes to past and future nonexistence are *as reasonable as* our asymmetrical attitudes to past and future pains and pleasures.

It might seem that one way to account for this asymmetry between our attitudes to past and future nonexistence, past and future pain and pleasure, is to see them as

---

[16] Robert Nozick, *Philosophical Explanations* (Cambridge, Mass.: Harvard University Press, 1981), pp. 744-745. However Nozick acknowledges that the example comes originally from Derek Parfit, whose own version is now available in his *Reasons and Persons*, pp. 165-166.

[17] Nozick, p. 745.

[18] Of course, it may still be that, as Parfit suggests (pp. 176-177), it would be *better* for us not to be biased toward the future in that we would then be happier about aging and the approach of death.

special cases of a general asymmetry in our attitudes to the past and the future. The past is closed whereas the future is open. Regret about what is done and gone is pointless ("it's no use crying over spilt milk") while the future contains genuine open possibilities and hence it is reasonable to regard it differently. However in the case of death, though the future is open in that many possible paths open up before us, yet they will all arrive at the same place — death. Thus if there's no point in crying over spilt milk, there's also no point in crying over milk that's sure to be spilt. Now I've argued that it is nevertheless reasonable to fear, as it were, that milk might be spilt tomorrow when you would prefer it at least not to be spilt until the day after that. This is because of the way that a death which is premature with regard to the fulfilment of some interest can harm the interest that our future-directed desires have created. And this in turn connects with the more general point that our asymmetrical attitudes to past and future reflect our fundamental mode of existence as goal-directed agents.

VIII

At this point it also seems worth remarking upon another argument Lucretius presents. It is to the effect that since you are going to be dead the same time (i.e. infinity) whenever you die, you ought to be indifferent whether you die sooner or later (*De Rerum Natura*, III, 1090-4). Of course, I have already argued that a premature death can thwart my interests and thus harm me. In that case it is reasonable to wish to die later if I have certain interests that will remain unfulfilled otherwise. However there are also other objections that can be raised to Lucretius's argument here. In the first place Bernard Williams has urged that there is an *ad hominem* difficulty for this argument:

> For it must imply that if there *were* a finite period of death, such that if you died later you would be dead for less time, then there *would* be some point in wanting to die later rather than earlier.[19]

---

[19] Williams, p. 84.

But this in turn implies that being dead is somehow an undesirable condition, which the Epicureans deny. In other words, Lucretius is arguing that no matter when you die you are dead the same time (i.e. infinity) and thus the evil of being dead is the same in each case. But Lucretius is already committed to denying that death is an evil. However it surely isn't necessary to see this argument as contradicting Epicurean principles. Rather it is more plausible to interpret it as a hypothetical argument which points out that, even if death were an evil, no matter when you died you would still have the same amount of this evil (i.e. infinity) and so it is unreasonable to fear to die sooner rather than later. That is, if (*per impossibile*) death is an evil, any time you die the evil is equal.

However Williams also presents a second argument against Lucretius that seems much stronger. Let's begin with the obvious objection to Lucretius: Although we may be dead the same time no matter when we die, we're not alive the same time. But what do we mean by this? Is it perhaps that since life is a good then, other conditions being equal, more of it is better than less? But this will hardly satisfy Lucretius who denies that life is a good because there is no possible contrasting evil. Rather life is a precondition for other goods (and evils). However it does seem that more of these other goods are certainly better than less, other conditions being equal. And so it seems also to follow that a life characterized by longer enjoyment of these goods is preferable to one characterized by shorter enjoyment of them. In other words, given equally good quality of life, a longer life is preferable to a shorter one and thus it should not be a matter of indifference to us when we die.

IX

Most philosophers who have concerned themselves with the question of death have been at least partially motivated by a desire to alleviate the fear that death so often inspires.[20] The Epicurean arguments we have been considering are clearly so motivated. They seek to liberate us from the fear of death by exposing the irrationality

---

[20] For a survey of what the major Western philosophers have said about death see Jacques Choron, *Death and Western Thought* (New York: Macmillan, 1963).

of this fear. Similarly the later Stoics also sought in their way to liberate us from the fear of death by urging that we see it as part of the natural order and by thinking of it constantly, reconcile ourselves to it. Both the Epicureans and the Stoics thus recommend that we conquer our fear of death by facing it squarely and dwelling upon it until we see its baselessness (Epicurus, Lucretius) or alternatively its ungraciousness (Seneca compares an unwillingness to quit life gracefully with an unwillingness to rise from a banquet at the appointed time). Another kind of solution to the fear of death is Spinoza's who recommends we concern ourselves with life rather than death. In a well known passage in his *Ethics* (IV, prop. LXVII) he says:

> A free man, that is to say, a man who lives acording to the dictates of reason alone, is not led by the fear of death, but directly desires the good; that is to say, desires to act, to live, and to preserve his being in accordance with the principle of seeking his own profit. He thinks, therefore, of nothing less than of death, and his wisdom is a meditation upon life.[21]

Hence from the Epicureans, the Stoics and Spinoza we gain the impression that the fear of death is an unreasonable one unworthy of the true philosopher.

I have argued, on the other hand, that the Epicureans fail to establish that fearing death is unreasonable and I have further claimed that the fear of death is indeed reasonable. This apparently places me in opposition not only to the Epicureans but also to the Stoics and to Spinoza. Nevertheless I think that our positions may be closer than they might at first appear. I want to try to bring this out by asking what it is for a fear to be unreasonable.

Suppose I fear being painfully gored by a unicorn when next I go for a walk in the park. This fear is clearly unreasonable because there is no reason to believe that unicorns exist. The fear has no "object" as it were. But the fear of death cannot be unreasonable in this sense because no one wants to claim that the phenomenon of death does not exist. Suppose instead then that I fear that when driving my car I will be involved in an accident and badly injured. This is not an unreasonable fear in that the

---

[21] Benedict de Spinoza, *Ethic.* 4th ed., trans. W. H. White & A. H. Sterling (London: Oxford University Press, 1930), p. 235.

phenomenon of traffic accidents unfortunately exists. Moreover, statistically I am likely to be involved in at least one accident in the course of a driving career. Indeed many motorists consider such a fear reasonable enough to take out accident insurance on themselves. Suppose, however, that I carried my reasonable fear of traffic accidents through to the extent of not driving at all and finally to the extent of never crossing a road lest I be knocked down by a car. In the end I just sit in my house and refuse to set foot outside the door. This is clearly an unreasonable fear. It is unreasonable not because its "object" (traffic accidents) does not exist — they certainly do occur. Nor is it primarily unreasonable because of the unlikeliness of being involved in an accident. Rather it is unreasonable because it frustrates all the agent's other purposes. Such an agent is, as Spinoza puts it, "led by the fear of death" so that he is unable any longer to seek what is useful to him. This is how a reasonable fear of death might easily become an unreasonable one and I suggest that a concern with this possibility has motivated quite dissimilar positions on the topic of the fear of death. In their different ways the Epicureans, the Stoics and Spinoza are all trying to prevent the fear of death paralysing our actions, for such a fear would be irrational in the sense of self-defeating to the agent's purposes and interests. (Indeed an agent who feared death that much should presumably be led to commit suicide to evade it.)

Now my argument for the reasonableness of fearing death turned upon the notion of death thwarting an agent's interests. But if an agent allows a reasonable fear of death to defeat the purposes he or she presumably wishes to be alive to pursue, then such a fear itself harms the agent's interests and becomes unreasonable.[22] In this sense my account leaves room for the fear of death to be in certain contexts an unreasonable one, though for the most part it would be reasonable enough. The conditions that if satisfied would make it an unreasonable fear have to do with whether the fear is one self-defeating to the agent's goals and purposes and harmful to his or her interests. Thus on a practical level I don't think my position is so dissimilarly motivated to that of the Epicureans, the Stoics and Spinoza for I have tried to do justice to the harm with

---

[22] For a similar suggestion see Jeffrie G. Murphy, "Rationality and the Fear of Death" *The Monist* **59** (1976): 187-203

which death threatens our future-directed interests, while also pointing out that an undue concern with death can harm these interests just as much.

The argument so far, however, now raises some more general concerns about how to live rationally in the face of death. In particular, there naturally arise certain traditional philosophical worries about the relation of death to the meaning and value of life. It is to these questions that I shall turn in the next chapter.

CHAPTER 4: DEATH AND THE MEANING OF LIFE

To live rationally one must live so that death cannot destroy life.
(Tolstoy, *What I Believe*, VIII)

Questions about the meaning of life have traditionally been regarded as being of particular concern to philosophers. However it is sometimes complained of contemporary analytic philosophy that it fails to address such questions. This charge is not really fair for there do exist illuminating recent discussions of these questions by analytic philosophers.[1] But perhaps what lurks behind this complaint is a feeling that these sorts of discussions are insufficiently close to the actual living situations that give rise to these questions and hence often seem rather thin and bland compared with the vivid portrayals of these situations in autobiography or fiction. With this suggestion in mind I want to focus on two works by the great Russian author Leo Tolstoy — one autobiographical, one fictional — and try to see what philosophical lessons can be learned from them, particularly with regard to questions about the relation of death to the meaning of life.[2]

Tolstoy's *A Confession* (1879) is a particularly interesting document for our purposes here for it is a vivid record of his own crisis connected with his search for the meaning of life. He tells how in middle life, in full possession of all his physical and mental powers, a happy man with family, wealth and fame, he suddenly suffered an "arrest of life" as he began to ask himself, "What is it for? What does it lead to?" (p. 15). And to these questions he could find no answer that satisfied him in the face of his

---

[1] See, for example, the selections in the anthology E. D. Klemke, ed., *The Meaning of Life* (New York: Oxford University Press, 1981) and the discussion in Robert Nozick, *Philosophical Explana tions* , Ch.6.

[2] References to Tolstoy's works are to the Maude translations in the Tolstoy Centenary Edition. In particular, volumes 11 and 15: *A Confession and The Gospel in Brief* (London: Oxford University Press, 1933) and *Ivan Ilych and Hadji Murad* (London: Oxford University Press, 1934). A useful general study of Tolstoy's ethico-religious views is Gordon William Spence, *Tolstoy the Ascetic* (Edinburgh: Oliver & Boyd, 1967).

own inevitable death. His family and his art, which had formerly been the centre of his life, could no longer provide meaning to life in the face of death:

> To-day or to-morrow sickness and death will come (they had come already)
> to those I love or to me; nothing will remain but stench and worms. Sooner
> or later my affairs whatever they may be, will be forgotten, and shall not
> exist. Then why go on making any effort? (pp. 19-20).

He studied science and philosophy hoping for some aid but to no avail. The experimental sciences seemed to him to refuse to acknowledge his problem, addressing themselves instead to their own independent questions. Philosophy, on the other hand, while recognizing his problem as legitimate seemed to have no answer. Indeed, as Tolstoy puts it, "though all the mental work is directed just to my question, there is no answer, but instead of an answer one gets the same question, only in a complex form" (p. 30). Hence the question he had posed himself remained unanswered: "Is there any meaning in my life that the inevitable death awaiting me does not destroy?" (p. 24).

In his despair it seemed to him that there are only four possible responses. The first is not understanding that life is absurd. But this was obviously not available to Tolstoy himself since "one cannot cease to know what one does know" (p. 39). The second, adopted by the majority of his circle, is "epicureanism", i.e. making the most of the pleasures of life while recognizing its ultimate hopelessness. But such conduct Tolstoy found himself unable to imitate, lacking the requisite "dullness of imagination". The third option is suicide and this seemed to Tolstoy the "worthiest way of escape" (p. 41). However it was the fourth way, that of "weakness", which he himself adopted. To his self-disgust he found himself "seeing the truth of the situation and yet clinging to life, knowing in advance that nothing can come of it" (p. 41).

At this point in his personal story Tolstoy's thoughts suddenly take a different turn:

The reasoning showing the vanity of life is not so difficult, and has long been familiar to the very simplest folk; yet they have lived and still live. How is it they all live and never think of doubting the reasonableness of life? (p. 43).

Thus he infers that "there is a whole humanity that lived and lives as if it understood the meaning of its life, for without understanding it it could not live" (p. 43). This led him to break away from his own narrow circle of social equals in order to attend to what the simple folk had to teach him. And this in turn led him to conclude that:

Rational knowledge, presented by the learned and the wise, denies the meaning of life, but the enormous masses of men, the whole of mankind, receive that meaning in irrational knowledge. And that irrational knowledge is faith (p. 47).

But in this conclusion he found no comfort for "it appears that in order to understand the meaning of life I must renounce my reason, the very thing for which alone a meaning is required" (p. 47). That is, though the problem of the meaning of life can only arise for a rational being, it is hardly a solution to it to abandon rationality.

In the face of this paradox he tries to clarify the distinction between "rational knowledge" and "irrational knowledge". In terms of rational knowledge he now recognizes why his question is unanswerable:

The solution of all the possible questions of life could evidently not satisfy me, for my question, simple as it at first appeared, included a demand for an explanation of the finite in terms of the infinite, and vice versa (p. 48).

The answers given by faith, however, though "irrational and distorted" attempt to provide such a relation between finite and infinite, which is unavailable through rational knowledge and yet "without which there can be no solution" (p. 49). Thus consider the catechism:

How am I to live? — According to the law of God. What real result will
come of my life? — Eternal torment or eternal bliss. What meaning has life
that death does not destroy? — Union with the eternal God: heaven (p. 50).

But faith is not to be identified with these propositional elements so far as Tolstoy
is concerned, for he admits these "answers" to be "irrational and distorted". Rather
"faith is a knowledge of the meaning of life in consequence of which man does not
destroy himself but lives" (p. 51).

Of course, though faith is not to be identified with these propositional elements,
they are nevertheless still involved. Thus Tolstoy says that "I was now ready to accept
any faith if only it did not demand of me a direct denial of reason — which would be a
falsehood" (pp. 53-54). But inevitably Tolstoy found himself confronted with rival
faiths and interpretations so that reason is once again introduced to arbitrate. This in
turn leads to his prolonged and serious study of the Gospels and theology.

Note that Tolstoy's position on faith is very much in keeping with modern non-
propositional accounts of revelation and faith.[3] Tolstoy is opposed to the traditional
propositional account that makes faith the acceptance of a body of propositional truths
which are not accessible to human reason. This view posits an evidential gap between
revealed truths and the truths of natural theology. And that in turn typically leads to an
emphasis on the role of the will in religious faith, for volitional response is supposed
to bridge the gap. Faith becomes the willing to believe something that cannot be
known through reason (Tolstoy's "irrational knowledge"). But this is not the view of
faith Tolstoy himself wants to embrace. Rather for him faith is an experiencing of the
world as significant. It is not therefore opposed to rational knowledge as it is on the
propositional account. While reason is not allowed to displace experience as the source
of the basic data, it is of course involved in the systematic formulation and criticism of
what is believed on the basis of faith. Faith, then, is a non-propositional knowledge of
how to live, though this knowledge may imply certain propositions that are open to

---

[3] For an account of modern developments along these lines see John Baillie, *The Idea of
Revelation in Recent Thought* (New York: Columbia University Press, 1956). An outstanding
philosophical defence of this non-propositional view is to be found in the writings of John Hick,
especially his *Faith and Knowledge* 2nd ed. (London: Macmillan, 1967).

rational criticism. This sort of account of faith has become widespread within Protestant Christianity this century and it indeed accords well with Tolstoy's own radically Protestant attitudes to scriptures and theology as expressed, for example, in his *What I Believe.*

This résumé of Tolstoy's argument is very brief and inevitably fails to capture the power of the original. However let us pause here to consider more closely two important philosophical points that arise. In the first place recall Tolstoy's claim that the peasants must understand the meaning of life, since without understanding it they could not carry on as they do. Now it might seem that there is no reason why the peasants should not just carry on and spend their time as Tolstoy had spent the first fifty years of his life, ignoring the suspicion that there is any problem about meaningfulness. But to this Tolstoy would presumably reply that the peasants lack the opportunities for diversion which enabled him to avoid facing the problem squarely for so long. Antony Flew, however, has challenged Tolstoy's original inference here on other grounds.[4] Flew suggests that though the peasants do not suffer from Tolstoy's "arrest of life", this does not imply that they possess some knowledge of life's meaning that Tolstoy does not. Rather Flew wants to invoke Ryle's distinction between knowing *how* and knowing *that.* Thus "the peasants may indeed know how to live their lives free of all sophisticated psychological disabilities, but this by no means presupposes the possession of any theoretical knowledge not vouchsafed to their unfortunate social superiors" (pp. 162-163). The secret that the peasants have and Tolstoy does not is not the knowledge *that* things are thus and thus, but rather the knowledge *how* to go on living. And in this case, Flew claims, this is "only another way of saying that they all enjoy rude mental health" (p. 164).

But this analysis is not fully convincing. First, though it is true that to know the meaning of life is to know *how* to live (as Tolstoy did not at the time of his crisis), yet it is not so clear that to admit this is to rule out the possibility that some knowledge *that* is nevertheless involved here. This is because of the epistemic point that knowledge how and knowledge that are not as entirely unrelated as Flew's analysis suggests. For

---

[4] Antony Flew, *The Presumption of Atheism* (London: Elek/Pemberton, 1976), Ch.12. (This chapter is a revised version of Flew's earlier paper "Tolstoi and the Meaning of Life" *Ethics* 73 (1963): 110-118.)

example, if I know how to speak Japanese this knowledge how need not be reducible to a set of knowledge that statements. Nonetheless the truth of the claim "I know *how* to speak Japanese fluently" generally implies the truth of other sentences like "I know *that* the Japanese word for cat is '*neko*'" and so on. Or again, if we think of knowledge how as knowledge of a technique (like the craftsman's knowledge) we generally imply that the knower has some understanding of the principles involved in the activity in question. He or she may not actually be able to articulate these principles in practice, but they are nevertheless theoretically formulable. In other words, knowing how implies some knowing that even if knowing how is not reducible to knowing that.

Nor will it do to weaken the sense of "knowing how" used here in order to try to save the analysis. As Ronald Hepburn acknowledges, there is a weak sense of "knowing how" used in ordinary language such that it is applicable to the baby who knows how to cry or even the bird that knows how to build a nest.[5] But this is not enough for Flew's analysis to hold. In the first place it is surely misleading to call these latter types of cases instances of knowing how at all. Rather we need to draw a distinction between knowing how to do something and being able to do it. It seems preferable to reserve "knowing how" for cases where the knower has some implicit understanding of the principles involved in the activity. Thus I am able to bend my forefinger but I do not know how to do this. Similarly animals are able to do many things but it seems reasonable to be agnostic about whether they know how to do these things. In the second place, even if we concede that this weak sense of "knowing how" is indeed knowing how, then we lose an important dimension of the problem that such "knowledge how" is being claimed to be the solution of. As Hepburn points out (pp. 215-216), the knowledge how that the peasants have on this interpretation of "knowing how" is no longer the knowledge Tolstoy was searching for, because their "knowledge" is too unproblematic to be a *solution* to his problem. It is the dimension of a problem struggled with and solved that is lacking in this case.

The second point I want to comment on in Tolstoy's account is the way in which he might seem to assume that the finality of death entails the meaninglessness of life. Once again Flew takes him to task for this, pointing out that it is by no means obvious

---

[5] R. W. Hepburn, "Questions About the Meaning of Life" in Klemke, p. 215.

that "nothing can matter unless it goes on forever; or, at any rate, eventually leads to something else which does" (p. 160). Now Flew is surely correct in saying that we value some things precisely because of their transitoriness: consider the Japanese cult of the cherry blossom. And again, think of Tolstoy's question "What for?" asked of activities like his work on his estate, or the education of his son, or the writing of a book (p. 16). If what is being assumed is that an intelligible justification for these activities must lie in something that goes on forever, something outside mortal life, then this is also wrong. Just how would Tolstoy's immortality have justified these activities? Furthermore, if these immediate activities can be called into question, then so too can any larger scheme of justification that is put forward as giving point to these activities.

But clearly Tolstoy was aware of this. Doesn't it indeed generate his crisis? So Flew is wrong to claim that Tolstoy contends that "our lives can have meaning only on the assumptions of the existence of God and of human immortality" (p. 154). The catechism from *A Confession*(p. 50) which Flew quotes is not Tolstoy's own view. Rather, as I already pointed out, it is offered as an illustration of the "irrational and distorted" replies given as propositions to be believed on faith, where "faith" is interpreted in the traditional propositional sense. Moreover in his later work *What I Believe* (Ch. VIII) Tolstoy denies that Christianity should involve any belief in physical resurrection and sternly renounces the idea that immortality is a necessary condition of the meaningfulness of life. Similarly Tolstoy's own doctrine of God is a rather thin demythologised one so that Flew himself notes that Tolstoy's faith is an idiosyncratically attenuated form of Christianity. Nor is Tolstoy guilty of any obvious muddles about the limits of explanation and justification; consider this passage towards the very end of *A Confession* where he tries to express the special character of the religious knowledge that gives meaning to life:

I shall not seek the explanation of everything. I know that the explanation of everything, like the commencement of everything, must be concealed in infinity. But I wish to understand in a way which will bring me to what is inevitably inexplicable. I wish to recognize anything that is inexplicable as being so not because the demands of my reason are wrong (they are right, and apart from them I can understand nothing), but because I recognize the limits of my intellect. I wish to understand in such a way that everything that is inexplicable shall present itself to me as being necessarily inexplicable and not as being something I am under an arbitrary obligation to believe (pp. 80-81).

Hence Flew's interpretation is too ungenerous a reading of Tolstoy's views on death and meaning. In *What I Believe* Tolstoy wisely remarks: "To live rationally one must live so that death cannot destroy life" (p. 430). *A Confession* records the experienced collapse of the supposed rationality of one man's life in the face of the realization of his own inevitable death. The life Tolstoy was living was one that death *would* defeat, built as it was upon attachment to his family and his art — attachments defeatible by death:

I felt that what I had been standing on had collapsed and that I had nothing left under my feet. What I had lived on no longer existed, and there was nothing left (p. 17).

The possibility of living a life not built upon attachment of this sort is the goal before us. And to know how to live such a life is to discover the meaning of life. That this seems platitudinous should not surprise us. The knowledge *that* involved in knowing the meaning of life may simply be some truth as unsurprising as this. This is why knowledge *that* is not sufficient to live meaningfully — we also have to know *how* to live in terms of this knowledge *that*. There is a parallel here with our experience of art. When pressed to say what it is that we feel we have learned from a work of art we often can only come up with some platitude. We find we can only say we now know that p, where p is some proposition we surely already knew to be the case. But perhaps what we are sometimes trying to say is that although we already knew *that p*, now we know *how* to operate with our knowledge that. If this is so then it is no accident that many of these matters are illuminated for us in Tolstoy's great story *The Death of Ivan Ilych* (1886).[6]

---

[6] There is an interesting philosophical discussion of this story in İlham Dilman and D. Z. Phillips, *Sense and Delusion* (London: Routledge & Kegan Paul, 1971).

In *A Confession* Tolstoy tells how his questions, "What is it for? What does it lead to?" seemed at first of no real relevance. But their continual reappearance began eventually to disturb him: "like drops of ink always falling on one place they ran together into one black blot" (p. 16). He immediately follows this simile with a striking passage:

> Then occurred what happens to everyone sickening with a mortal internal disease. At first trivial signs of indisposition appear to which the sick man pays no attention; then these signs reappear more and more often and merge into one uninterrupted period of suffering. The suffering increases and, before the sick man can look round, what he took for a mere indisposition has already become more important to him than anything else in the world — it is death! (p. 16).

The prefiguring of *The Death of Ivan Ilych* is remarkable. *The Death of Ivan Ilych* tells of a man suffering from a fatal illness who sees that in the face of his imminent death the life he has led is to be judged meaningless. Although it is Ivan's life that the story presents for us, it is also quite clear that his case is to be viewed as an entirely typical one: "Ivan Ilych's life had been most simple and most ordinary and therefore most terrible" (p. 11). Appropriately he had been a member of the Court of Justice and, as he had judged others, so he is forced to come to judge himself. His life had been a story of steady and reliable progress in his own sphere of government legal appointments. He had always done his duty as it was expected of him, for "he considered his duty to be what was so considered by those in authority" (p. 12). In turn he expects that those in authority will similarly do their duty by him and steadily promote him. And this expectation is duly satisfied. Although he briefly suffers one unpleasant setback in his career expectations, in his eyes order is soon restored and he is appointed to the position of power he sees as his due: "after a stumble, his life was regaining its due and natural character of pleasant lightheartedness and decorum" (p. 24). But at the height of his triumph he suffers an apparently trivial accident — "he made a false step and slipped" (p. 26) — that brings on an internal illness which eventually proves fatal. He is confined to bed and forced to confront his imminent death. And in the face of this he realizes that the life he has led is empty.

When Ivan first realizes that he is indeed dying his reaction is one of despair for "not only was he not accustomed to the thought, he simply did not and could not grasp it" (p. 44). Although he must have known that he was to die some time, he has never really lived in terms of that knowledge. Death is something that happens to other people:

> The syllogism he had learnt from Kiezewetter's Logic: "Caius is a man, men are mortal, therefore Caius is mortal", had always seemed to him correct as applied to Caius, but certainly not as applied to himself. That Caius — man in the abstract — was mortal, was perfectly correct, but he was not Caius, not an abstract man, but a creature quite quite separate from all others (pp. 44-45).

Ironically in the opening pages of the story we see Ivan's one-time colleagues treating Ivan's own death in an identical fashion, complacent that "it is he who is dead and not I" (p. 2). Thus Schwartz winks at Peter Ivanovich "as if to say: 'Ivan Ilych has made a mess of things — not like you and me'" (p. 3). And Peter Ivanovich sees in the expression on the corpse's face a warning to the living that seems "out of place, or at least not applicable to him" (p. 5). When told of Ivan's terrible sufferings in his last days Peter Ivanovich pauses for an instant:

> "Three days of frightful suffering and then death! Why, that might suddenly, at any time, happen to me," he thought, and for a moment felt terrified. But — he did not himself know how — the customary reflection at once occurred to him that this had happened to Ivan Ilych and not to him, and that it should not and could not happen to him ... After which reflection Peter Ivanovich felt reassured, and began to ask with interest about the details of Ivan Ilych's death, as though death was an accident natural to Ivan Ilych but certainly not to himself (p. 9).

This is the spirit of deception that screened Ivan from his own death until it was imminent and caused his family to try to deny that his dying was really happening:

The awful terrible act of his dying was, he could see, reduced by those about him to the level of a casual, unpleasant, and almost indecorous incident (as if someone had entered a drawing-room diffusing an unpleasant odour) and this was done by that very decorum which he had served all his life long (pp. 51-52).

The only exception to this falsity, this refusal to recognize death as inevitable for everyone, is the peasant lad Gerasim who serves Ivan in his last days. It is Gerasim who reminds Peter Ivanovich at the beginning of the story: "It's God's will. We shall all come to it some day" (p. 11). And it is Gerasim who says frankly to Ivan:

"We shall all of us die, so why should I grudge a little trouble?" — expressing the fact that he did not think his work burdensome, because he was doing it for a dying man and hoped someone would do the same for him when his time came (p. 52).

But for Ivan, whose whole way of life has screened him from having to face this truth about death, dying is an incomprehensible and terrible business. He comes to realize that the life he had felt to be so pleasant is in fact "something trivial and often nasty" (p. 63). As he looks back on his life it begins to seem to him that only in his childhood is there something worthwhile. Everything else is a gradual decline:

It is as if I had been going downhill while I imagined I was going up. And that is really what it was. I was going up in public opinion, but to the same extent life was ebbing away from me. And now it is all done and there is only death (p. 64).

In the face of this realization Ivan experiences life as "senseless and horrible" and in terror searches for some meaning to it all. Then he glimpses something:

"Maybe I did not live as I ought to have done," it suddenly occurred to him. "But how could that be, when I did everything properly?" he replied, and immediately dismissed from his mind this, the sole solution of all the riddles of life and death, as something quite impossible (p. 64).

It takes Ivan quite some time to admit that his flawlessly correct life is not the life he ought to have lived, to see that "all that for which he had lived ... was not real at all, but a terrible and huge deception which had hidden both life and death" (p. 69). As he resists this notion he screams, "I won't" and then just, "Oh! Oh! Oh!" as he feels himself being forcibly thrust into a black hole. The screaming continues for three days until on the third day he stops:

"Yes, it was all not the right thing," he said to himself, "but that's no matter. It can be done. But what *is* the right thing?" he asked himself, and suddenly grew quiet (p. 72).

At this point he becomes aware of the suffering he is causing his family as he catches sight of his distraught son and wife. Then the answer to his question, "What *is* the right thing?" becomes clear:

And suddenly it grew clear to him that what had been oppressing him and would not leave him was all dropping away at once from two sides, from ten sides, and from all sides. He was sorry for them, he must act so as not to hurt them: release them and free himself from these sufferings (p. 73).

And now "in place of death there was light". Ivan says to himself, "Death is finished ... It is no more!" and he dies.

Ivan had built his life upon attachments defeatible by death. This is why he suffers so much in the face of death, for what he has lived for is rendered meaningless by death:

This is wrong, it is not as it should be. All you have lived for and still live for is falsehood and deception, hiding life and death from you (p. 70).

His life had been built upon his desire for control and power. Hence his distress at minor flaws in the environment he has created — a stained tablecloth, a chipped plate, a scratched table, or even the way his daughter's hair is done (pp. 27, 31, 47). His increasing concern with his illness results in a corresponding sensitivity to any lack of control:

He had formerly borne such mischances, hoping soon to adjust what was wrong, to master it and attain success, or make a grand slam. But now every mischance upset him and plunged him into despair (p. 35).

But it is the letting go of such control that is required. Death inevitably defeats such control and the attempt to hold on to it in the face of death causes Ivan terrible suffering. It is only when he recalls the suffering of his family and desires to "release them and free himself from these sufferings" (p. 73) that the fear of death leaves him. Then "in place of death there was light". Until then the kind of life he has led has screened him from the reality of death and the way in which it will destroy all he has built his life on. When he glimpses this truth about death he is horrified and resists this knowledge. But eventually he admits it, together with the associated judgement of the meaninglessness of the life he has led. He considers not himself and his control and power, but other people. Having forgone this old desire for control and power, he can say to himself, "Death is finished ... It is no more", for now death cannot defeat him.

How does this connect with our original questions about death and the meaning of life? First, it is the knowledge of death that once again gener ates the crisis. Ivan (like any adult human) must know *that* he will die but since he refuses to face this fact, he has no idea of how to live in the light of it. He does not know *how* to live. In the face of his death he comes to know that the way he has lived is wrong, for his death renders meaningless the life he has led by destroying that to which he is so attached: viz. power and control. Once again it is the peasants who provide us with a positive paradigm. In this case it is Gerasim, who knows that he will die as will we all and who knows how to live in terms of this knowledge. He does not grudge Ivan his services but just sees them as what is needed by a dying man and hopes some day someone will do the same for him.

Secondly, note that the meaningfulness or meaninglessness of life is not assumed to be dependent upon the prospect of immortality. Tolstoy is careful to leave the question of survival after death completely open. The imagery of light is entirely compatible with a naturalistic reading of the story: Ivan is enlightened as he turns from the darkness of deception and falsehood. Again, consider the point in the story when Ivan attempts to ask his family's forgiveness and fails to mouth the words properly. Nonetheless he is content "knowing that He whose understanding mattered would understand" (p. 73). But this does not commit Tolstoy to the belief that for Ivan's life to be meaningful there must exist a God. It is entirely consistent with the point of the story that this is simply a statement about Ivan's beliefs, not an affirmation of the truth of the claim that there is a such a "He". Nor need it suggest that such a *belief* is necessary for a person to consider his or her life meaningful. Ivan's conviction can be understood in a hypothetical or even a counterfactual sense, i.e. if there is such a He then He will understand. This point in turn connects with another that arises in response to the following possible objection.

So far I have argued that Tolstoy does not commit the crude error that Flew attributes to him: viz. that if something is to be worthwhile it must last forever or lead to something that does. However perhaps Tolstoy does tacitly assume another and rather similar principle which is less absurd, though it may likewise be false. Tolstoy suggests that death robs life (or a certain kind of life) of its meaning. Does it follow that life is meaningless? Not necessarily. Consider the thesis that one thing of value is pleasure. Then life has value while it is pleasurable and sickness and death take away that value. However they do not render life valueless *while* it is pleasurable. It is only when the pleasure ceases that it lacks value. To get the desired conclusion something like the following principle is required: that if a thing has value at a certain moment of time then it always has that value (or at all later times). And this principle is in turn plausible because it suffers from an ambiguity. If pleasure (or being in a pleasurable state) is intrinsically valuable then it is eternally true (presumably) that pleasure has that value. However my life has value only because it *instances* such states with value. And it has this value only while it does instance those states. Thus valuable states are eternally valuable, whereas things which instance those states enjoy the value only while they enjoy the states. Now apply the principle wrongly construed to my life. If it has a certain value then it will always have it. However the value that pleasure bestows on my life is obviously robbed by death. So my life never has that value, even while it is pleasurable.

If Tolstoy is playing with such a principle then he may be in trouble for then life could be meaningful only if either: (i) it instances valuable or meaning-conferring states eternally (and this seems to imply the necessity of immortality); or (ii) there are some states which though transiently instanced confer eternal significance on a life. Tolstoy wants to eschew (i) so he must embrace (ii). And clearly he does think there are such states — perhaps those states instanced by those who live out the spirit of the gospels. How do these differ from pleasure? Undoubtedly they do, but it is not clear why. Why are Florence Nightingale's compassionate acts *still* significant or valuable, whereas Nero's pleasures are not?

In reply to this we need first to note that meanings are sought for lives as wholes. Lives (like stories) can have significance and value that are more than just the significance and value of their parts. Secondly, we need to draw a distinction between what I'll call the "objective" meaning of a life and the "subjective" meaning.[7] (This terminology need not commit us to any particular position on the objectivity or subjectivity of value in general.) A life can have subjective meaning insofar as it instances states of value for the person whose life it is. Thus pleasure can confer subjective meaning on a life in this way, though sickness and death will rob a life of

---

[7] It should be clear that this distinction is not equivalent to Nagel's distinction between subjective and objective discussed in Chapter 2. My distinction between subjective and objective values is probably closer to the distinction Nagel draws between agent-relative and agent-neutral values. However, in the first place, it is important to note that for Nagel both agent-relative and agent-neutral values are (in his sense) *objective*, since both can be understood from outside of the viewpoint of the individual for whom they are values. (Cf. his "The Limits of Objectivity", pp. 101-103.) Moreover it is not even clear that my notion of subjective and objective is equivalent to Nagel's agent-relative and agent-neutral, for the account I am offering is compatible with the possibility that all value is agent-relative—a possibility Nagel rejects.

such subjective meaning — not in the sense of making it no longer eternally true that the life instanced pleasure at some time, but rather in the sense that the life does not now instance pleasure. And this devaluation of a life is quite compatible with the truth that this does not render the life valueless while it is pleasurable. If a life as a whole is only subjectively meaningful its value ceases when the life ends. However a life can also have objective value insofar as it instances states of value for others and death does not destroy such value in the way it destroys subjective value. Personal pleasure can only have subjective value in this sense and this is why Nero's pleasures are no longer significant since Nero's death. Other states like compassion can instance value for others and hence not be devalued by death as are subjectively valuable states like pleasure. Thus Florence Nightingale's acts outlive her.

Now worries about the meaning of life are typically worries about how to integrate both senses of "meaning"; that is, to live a life which instances objective meaning that is not destroyed by death and also to enjoy such a life as affording subjective satisfaction to the person who leads it. In the case of Ivan Ilych the life he led before his illness was one that instanced only subjective meaning.[8] It was built upon the values of "pleasant light heartedness and decorum" (p. 24). He had been able to incorporate temporary disvalues precisely because he had always believed things would soon be restored to their even tenor. But death brings home to him the realization that the subjective meaning his life has cannot guarantee objective meaning for it and such subjective meaning as it has will be destroyed by his death.

---

[8] Someone might object that instancing subjective meaning is alone sufficient for a life to be meaningful. But consider this example from Robert Nozick's "On the Randian Argument" (*The Personalist* **52** (1971): 298):

> ...suppose we read the biography of a man who *felt* happy, took pride in his work, family life, etc. But we also read that his children, secretly, despised him; his wife, secretly, scorned him, having innumerable affairs; his work was a subject of ridicule among all others, who kept their opinion from him; *every* source of satisfaction in this man's life was built upon a falsehood, a deception. Do you, in reading about this man's life think: "What a *wonderful* life. I wish I, or my children, could lead it?" And don't say that you wouldn't want to lead the life because all the deceptions and falsehoods might come out making the man unhappy. They didn't. Of course, it is difficult to imagine the others behaving appropriately, and the person himself not being nagged by doubts. But is *this* the ground of one's reaction? Was it a good life? Does it lack *happiness*?

It might seem a consequence of this view that objective meaning is dependent upon the existence of others. This in turn will pose a difficulty if we consider the life of the last human agent. What would confer objective significance upon it? And if objective significance cannot be conferred upon it, does this retrospectively undercut the objective value of other lives? One possibility is that God provides the last human life with objective value. (This view has a certain Berkeleian flavour.) But then what provides God's existence with objective value? Of course His eternal existence together with His omnipotence guarantee the subjective value of His existence cannot be destroyed. So perhaps the problem of integrating objective and subjective value just does not arise for God. However another possibility is that the objective value of the last human life can be guaranteed in a counterfactual sense. That is, if there were others they would find it objectively meaningful. (God's existence could be objectively meaningful in the same way.) And this ties in with my earlier suggestion that we might interpret Ivan's conviction that "He whose understanding mattered would understand" (p. 73) in a counterfactual sense without disvaluing the objective meaningfulness of his life.

Understanding the meaning of life, then, does indeed involve knowledge how. But in relation to death it also involves, (as knowledge how generally does), knowledge that. In this case the knowledge that we will all die ought to lead us to the obvious conclusion that it would be irrational to build our lives on what can be destroyed by death. *A Confession* and *The Death of Ivan Ilych* record instances of men coming to the knowledge that their lives are so built and hence rendered meaningless by death. Knowing how to live a life not so built, knowing how to integrate the subjective and objective significance of a life, is what is involved in understanding the meaning of life. An important part of such knowledge how, (a part Tolstoy dwells upon to great effect), is the knowledge that we will all die and that "to live rationally one must live so that death cannot destroy life." Tolstoy sees the peasants like Gerasim as having such knowledge. As to the prospects of others gaining such knowledge, Tolstoy seems pessimistic. Ivan gains it only after terrible suffering and too late for him to do more than die well. And at the start of the story we see Ivan's family and colleagues have learned nothing from his death. Presumably the only hope is that it is the reader of the story who might learn something from Ivan's death. Indeed it might well turn out in the end that the "He" of the last chapter will be the reader, the person who Tolstoy hoped would understand.

PART TWO:

IMMORTALITY

CHAPTER 5: IMMORTALITY

I

Would personal immortality have any value for one so endowed? An affirmative answer would seem so obvious to some that they might be tempted to go so far as to claim that immortality is a condition of life's having any value at all. The claim that immortality is a *necessary* condition for the meaningfulness of life seems untenable (as we saw in the last chapter). What, however, of the claim that immortality is a *sufficient* condition for the meaningfulness of life? Though some might hold this to be the characteristic *religious* view, this is certainly disputable. Thus McTaggart reminds us, for instance, that "Buddhism ... holds immortality to be the natural state of man, from which only the most perfect can escape."[1] I want to argue that we can imagine variants of personal immortality which would not be valuable and hence immortality in itself cannot be a sufficient condition for value. What is required for the meaningfulness of life is that life exhibit certain valuable qualities. But then the endless exhibition of these qualities is not only unnecessary for the meaningfulness of life, but the endlessness of a life can even devalue those qualities that would make valuable a single, bounded life.

II

Before turning to this task, however, I want to consider a different sort of approach to the question of the relation between immortality and value. This consists in the claim that immortality is somehow a presupposition of our conceptions of value. This claim has been supported by various arguments. John Hick, for example, presents "the basic religious argument for immortality" as follows.[2] True, a humanist view of

[1] J. M. E. McTaggart, *Some Dogmas of Religion* (London: Edward Arnold, 1906), p. 278.

[2] John Hick, *Death and Eternal Life* (London: Collins, 1976), Ch. 8.

death is compatible with an optimistic view of life insofar as some exceptional figures like Hume can successfully fuse the two together in their own lives. However such a possibility is realizable only for the fortunate few. Most humans are deprived of the opportunity of realizing their potential. Thus for most the realization of this potential would require some form of continued personal life after death. In denying the reality of an afterlife, humanism is committed to the view that for the vast majority existence is in the end irredeemably tragic. The stark fact of the enormity of human suffering through the ages presents the humanist with a problem: is this all sheer, meaningless, unredeemed and unredeemable suffering? Hick sees three ways to evade this possibility and justify this suffering. First, to say that this is all God's will. As Paul puts it (Romans 9:20-21): "Will what is moulded say to its moulder, 'Why have you made me thus?' Has the potter no right over the clay?" This is an attempt at a religious justification which does not require human immortality. Second, to try to justify this suffering in terms of a future state that will evolve out of this painful process. (For an example of such an attempt consider Teilhard de Chardin's picture of the evolution of man into a "harmonized collectivity of consciousnesses equivalent to a sort of super-consciousness.")[3]

But Hick rejects both of these possibilities on moral grounds. They seem to treat persons as means rather than ends, to devalue the individual's moral status in favour of some future state in which the individual *himself* will not participate. Thus Hick opts for a third possibility and suggests we can justify this suffering in terms of a future state in which the individuals who suffered *themselves* participate. This is the Christian view of life: not a tragedy, but a divine comedy leading to a fulfilment which presupposes our continued existence after death. This is Hick's "basic religious argument for immortality".

The argument is, of course, uncompelling. In the first place it doesn't show that *immortality* is a requisite for justifying suffering. All that is required by the argument is sufficient post-mortem existence to balance up the inequalities. Secondly, Hick offers no argument to block the possibility of human suffering being unjustifiable. It may be that a tragic view of life is the appropriate one given the facts.

---

[3] Pierre Teilhard de Chardin, *The Phenomenon of Man* (London: Collins, 1959), p. 251.

Hick's allusion to the Kantian ethical doctrine that persons ought to be treated as ends and not means recalls to mind an ancestor of this sort of argument for immortality. In the *Critique of Practical Reason* (Bk. II, Ch. II, Sec. IV) Kant argues that immortality is a postulate of practical reason, a presupposition of morality. The argument goes as follows. In Kant's view the highest good (*summum bonum*) is the ideal union of moral perfection and complete happiness. This is the goal of practical reason and the possibility of this highest good is demanded by morality. Hence whatever must be presupposed to allow for this possibility is a practically reasonable postulate. Human immortality (together with human freedom and the existence of God) is such a postulate. In the case of immortality this is supposed to follow from the fact that the *summum bonum* is not actually achieved in the observable span of human life. Nevertheless the possibility of the highest good is practically necessary. Thus it is morally reasonable to suppose that human life extends beyond death in order to provide time for the required adjustment between virtue and happiness. Moreover, the argument continues, the finite agent's quest for moral perfection is inherently endless. Progress in virtue can continue *ad infinitum*. Thus it is necessary to postulate an endless duration within which this progress can take place. As Kant puts it, "the highest good is practically possible only on the supposition of the immortality of the soul, and the latter, as inseparably bound to the moral law, is a postulate of pure practical reason."[4] Kant concedes, of course, that immortality is "not as such demonstrable", not a matter of knowledge. However, it is one of our most profoundly reasonable beliefs.

Kant's argument clearly rests upon his moral theory and as such is vulnerable to attack in this direction. However there are also other ways in which the argument can be resisted. Firstly, we could deny that we are under any obligation to *attain* the highest good; we are only obliged to *strive towards* this unrealizable end. Secondly, the postulation of immortality cannot in itself guarantee the attainment of the ultimate moral goal so long as the autonomy of the agent is retained. Finally, the postulate won't really satisfy the practical need for the highest good's achievement. Recall that

---

[4] Immanuel Kant, *Critique of Practical Reason*, trans. Lewis White Beck (Indianapolis: Bobbs-Merrill, 1956), p. 127.

Kant insists on the endlessness of the afterlife in order to accommodate the infinitely progressive character of virtue. That is, moral perfection remains an unachievable goal. But then immortality is merely the indefinite postponement of the state of affairs demanded by practical reason. What is gained by introducing the *eternal* frustration of the highest good? Why not admit the unachievability of the ideal and abandon any claims to its obligatory character? Since the afterlife will not supply what morality supposedly demands, what warrant do we have for postulating immortality?

A different sort of argument from the conservation of value to immortality utilizes the "degrees of perfection" principle.[5] Ordinary human life is characteristically imperfect and incomplete. Hence the perfection of humans would typically require an afterlife. But the possibility of perfection is not merely a presupposition of value, for the ability to recognize degrees of perfection implies that perfection exists. Thus immortality is in turn implied. This argument has some resemblance to Aquinas' Fourth Way (*Summa Theologiae* Ia, 2,3) in that both utilize the "degrees of perfection" principle.[6] Aquinas begins from the fact that we observe a gradation of things such that some things are more or less good, or true, or noble etc. But comparative terms describe varying degrees of approximation to a superlative, i.e. things are said to be more or less F insofar as they approach what is most F. Therefore there is something which is the truest and best and noblest of things and hence most fully in being. Moreover, whatever is most F is the cause of whatever else is F, just as fire is the cause of hot things. Hence there is something that is the cause of being and goodness and any perfection in all things. This, Aquinas concludes, we call "God".

Both arguments appeal, then, to the principle that the admission of comparative claims like "Some things are better than others" commits us to the actual existence of a maximal exemplar of goodness. This Platonic assumption is entirely resistable. From the fact that superlative terms can be defined in terms of comparative terms, nothing significant can be inferred as to the existence of an exemplar of the superlative. Thus

---

[5] Cf. J. A. Harvie, "The Immortality of the Soul" *Religious Studies* 5 (1969): 219-220.

[6] Cf. also the proof from goodness in Anselm's *Monologian*, Ch. 4. This passage might plausibly be seen as an argument for what Augustine merely asserts in *The City of God* (Bk. 12, Ch.1).

degrees of size do not imply that there exists a largest possible thing, except in the sense that there exists a *de facto* largest thing (i.e. if there exists anything, there exists a thing than which there is no larger).[7] Aquinas himself would concede this point with regard to the example of size since he believed that there can be nothing which is unlimited in size (*Summa Theologiae* Ia, 7, 3). He is only concerned that his principle about comparatives apply to perfections which involve absolutely no imperfections: "transcendental perfections" like truth, goodness, beauty etc. But even so restricted the principle is dubious for it requires the further premise that existence is a perfection. That is, if transcendentally perfect truth did not exist it would not be the perfect truth that is implied by comparative judgements. But since existence is not a perfection, the argument is unsound.

To sum up so far, then, we have seen no reason to suppose that the prospect of immortality is somehow a requisite of our conceptions of value. Let us now turn to the question of the value of personal immortality.

III

In discussing this question of whether personal immortality would have any value it is fairer not to load the dice by imagining, for example, an eternal future of hideous pointless pain. Clearly this is a disvalue but that does not show immortality to be a disvalue. Rather let's take as our paradigm case the ordinary life with its share of pain and pleasure, joy and sorrow, satisfaction and frustration. Now most people consider their lives worth living: they do not contemplate suicide, but rather attempt to prolong their lives (provided, of course, that conditions do not degenerate too badly). Nor do they generally regret having been born. If their lives are valuable to them in this way, would not the endless extension of them also have value? Let's consider this question by examining some possible scenarios of immortality, stipulating that the quality of

---

[7] My objection here assumes the universe to be a finite collection of objects, as Aquinas believed. Hence he rejects the suggestion that there can exist an unlimited number of things (except potentially): "All created things must be subject therefore to definite enumeration. Thus even a number of things that happens to be unlimited cannot actually exist" (*Summa Theologiae* Ia, 7, 4). If, however, the universe is unlimited there need not exist even a *de facto* largest thing.

life in these imaginary cases be comparable with the quality of life exhibited by an
ordinary mortal life that is considered worthwhile by the person living it.

One possibility is the endless extension of this life. Here, however, we
immediately see the importance of our stipulation about quality of life. Ordinary
mortal life displays a typical pattern of gradual senility attending aging. That this
pattern transposed onto an eternal scale would not be a blessing is well brought out in
the tale of the Struldbruggs in Swift's *Gulliver's Travels*.[8] When Gulliver first hears
of the immortal Struldbruggs he conceives of such a fate as an extraordinarily
fortunate one. He imagines how if he himself had been born such a one he would have
pursued the arts and sciences in the company of his fellow immortals, having "by
Thrift and Management" succeeded in the first two hundred years of his life in
supplying the wealth necessary for these cultured pursuits. His Luggnuggian hosts are
amused at his idealized picture and inform him that in fact the Struldbruggs pass their
time quite differently. By the time they are eighty they have "not only all the Follies
and Infirmities of other old Men, but many more which arose from the dreadful
Prospect of never dying" (p. 212). As their memories fail them they can no longer
remember even the names of things, while the diseases to which they are subject still
continue without increasing or diminishing. "They were," Gulliver recalls, "the most
mortifying Sight I ever beheld ... Besides the usual Deformities in extreme Old Age,
they acquired an additional Ghastliness in Proportion to their Number of Years" (p.
214). Gulliver's original naive expectations about the desirability of being an
immortal were based, his Luggnuggian hosts point out, on an unfounded assumption:

> That the System of Living contrived by me was unreasonable and unjust,
> because it supposed a Perpetuity of Youth, Health, and Vigour, which no
> Man could be so foolish to hope, however extravagant he might be in his
> Wishes. That, the Question therefore was not whether a Man would chuse to
> be always in the Prime of Youth, attended with Prosperity and Health; but

---

[8] Jonathan Swift, *Gulliver's Travels*, ed. Herbert Davis (Oxford: Basil Blackwell, 1959), pp. 207-
214.

how he would pass a perpetual Life under all the usual Disadvantages which old Age brings along with it (p. 211).

This difficulty can be eliminated by considering a different version of the endless extension of this life, a version that satisfies Gulliver's original assumption. Bernard Williams has offered an interesting discussion of such a possibility based upon Karel Čapek's play *The Makropulos Case*.[9] EM, the heroine of this scenario, is 342 years old. She swallowed an elixir of life and for 300 years has been 42. Her life has been frozen and with this unending life has come boredom. She refuses to take the elixir again and dies. Considering this case Williams plausibly locates two conditions that any worthwhile form of personal immortality must satisfy: (i) that it is *me* who survives forever; and (ii) that my eternal future life must be adequately related to the life I have led so far and the aims and values I presently hold.[10] (For brevity I shall refer to these two conditions as respectively "the identity condition" and "the adequacy condition".) The first condition is required to eliminate forms of "immortality" through one's children, one's deeds etc. that do not involve personal continuance. The second condition is vague, but inevitably so for it depends upon what sorts of aims and possibilities I envisage for myself as of now.

Now in the case of EM her life fails to satisfy the adequacy condition. Her problem is boredom: everything has lost its freshness and her life has "frozen up". This problem seems inherent in her version of immortality. Her life is just too closely tied up to what has gone before for it to offer any new challenges and rewards. Williams sees this failure to satisfy the adequacy condition as inevitable with such a version of immortality, i.e. an eternal life that is an indefinite extension of the present one. Even if the present life has value for me, the infinite extension of it need not.

---

[9] Bernard Williams, *Problems of the Self*, Ch. 6. The EM scenario discussed here is the one presented by Williams. However it differs from that found in Karel Čapek, *The Macropulos Secret*, authorised English translation by Paul Selver (London: Robert Holden & Co., 1927). There EM claims to be 337 years old (p. 170). She took the elixir at 16 (p. 179) but she is commonly taken to be about 30 (pp. 18, 169).

[10] Williams, p. 91.

IV

Anyway, it does seem true that boredom requires memory of previous experiences. (Not, of course, total recall but at least some degree of recall.) Hence consider instead another scenario of immortality, viz. Nietzsche's "eternal recurrence":

> This life as you now live it and have lived it, you will have to live once more and innumerable times more; and there will be nothing new in it, but every pain and every joy and every thought and sigh and everything unutterably small or great in your life will have to return to you, all in the same succession and sequence ... The eternal hourglass of existence is turned upside down again and again, and you with it, speck of dust![11]

How well does this possibility satisfy our identity and adequacy conditions? In the first place consider the identity condition. There are two possible and contrasting objections that immediately arise here. The first is that the series of identical lives envisaged means not the infinite repetition of one person's life but an infinite series of numerically distinct and hence different persons. The second objection concedes that the recurrence involves the same person but insists that this "sameness" entails that there is not an infinite series of distinct lives but only one life.

Neither objection, however, is overwhelming. The first objection assumes that a person (or at least her life) has a particular ontological status (like an individual) such that recurrence will involve duplication. But if we hold (as Nietzsche did) that a person is a pattern of actions and experiences, then the repetition of this sequence is all that is required for recurrence to occur. A person is repeatable just as is a melody (i.e. a sequence of tones). The second objection appeals, of course, to Leibniz's Identity of Indiscernibles: if two lives are identical in all respects there are not *two* lives but one. It is not (as with the first objection) that the other lives are not *mine*. Rather the point is that, since there is no addition to my present experience represented in the envisaged

---

[11] Friedrich Nietzsche, *The Gay Science*, trans. Walter Kaufmann (New York: Random House, 1974), sect. 341.

recurrence, it makes no sense to talk of *this* occurrence as distinct from any other exactly similar one. But this Leibnizian argument presupposes a Leibnizian account of time and space. On an absolutist account of space-time we can conceive of the possibility of two identical and numerically distinct lives occurring at different temporal points. True, the person involved in this recurrence cannot recognize that this repetition is taking place. But God (outside of space-time) could.

Another difficulty arises, however, when we consider that on this scenario the person involved can have no memory of her previous lives — necessarily, since otherwise the memory of her last life would make her different from her immediate predecessor who could not have any memory of a life she had not yet lived. But with no memory of "my" previous lives, will it be *me* who lives them? Of course, personal identity can survive memory gaps in one life. Can it also survive life to life memory gaps? Surely it can, particularly if we understand the notion of identity here not so much in the strongest metaphysical sense but in a looser sense. That is, a sense such that personal identity is a relative notion, a matter of degree. This is what Derek Parfit calls the "complex view" about personal identity.[12] On this view the identities of persons are rather like the identities of nations. What is involved are certain continuities; psychological and bodily in the case of personal identity. Survival is a matter of degree. A life can be viewed as a succession of selves with no underlying, persisting person. The connections between past and future selves are connections of similarity, a relation that admits of degrees.

The importance of these weaker connections of similarity (perfect similarity in the case of eternal recurrence) can be highlighted by the consideration of the thought-experiment of choosing such a recurrence. Now on a practical level it seems

---

[12] See "Personal Identity" *Philosophical Review* **80** (1971): 3-27; "On 'The Importance of Self-Identity'" *Journal of Philosophy* **68** (1971): 683-690; "Later Selves and Moral Principles" in Alan Montefiore ed., *Philosophy and Personal Relations* (Montreal: McGill-Queen's University Press, 1973), pp. 137-169; and *Reasons and Persons*, Part Three. For the contrary claim that only the "simple view" of personal identity can satisfy our hopes and fears about immortality see Richard Swinburne, "Personal Identity" *Proceedings of the Aristotelian Society* **74** (1973-4): 231-247; and "Persons and Personal Identity" in H. D. Lewis ed., *Contemporary British Philosophy, Fourth Series* (London: George Allen & Unwin, 1976), pp. 221-237.

reasonable to avoid future pain even if there is no memory connection between present and future selves. This is well brought out by Peirce:

> "If the power to remember dies with the material body, has the question of any single person's future life after death any particular interest for him?" ... Now if we had a drug which would abolish memory for a while, and you were going to be cut for the stone, suppose the surgeon were to say, "You will suffer damnably, but I will administer this drug so that you will during that suffering lose all memory of your previous life. Now you have of course no particular interest in your sufferings as long as you will not remember your present and past life, you know, have you?"[13]

Pragmatically speaking it appears that psychological continuities between present and future selves are sufficient to ground emotional empathy for, or a practical egoistic decision concerning the future self, even if metaphysically it is not identical with the present self but rather a duplicate.

So much for the identity condition then. What of the adequacy condition? There is, of course, no memory of having lived this life before so no boredom of EM's type is possible. Nevertheless, even if I won't be bored in her manner, my life will still be frozen in that it will be endlessly repeated. Does this repetitiveness matter? Does it violate the adequacy condition? One possible difficulty that could seem to arise is that eternal recurrence seems incompatible with goal-oriented life planning. If a life is thought to have meaning insofar as it approaches a particular goal, then (given eternal recurrence) either that goal can never occur, or it has already occurred an infinite number of times. But to meet this objection we can relativize the notion of goal such that each iterated transformation has a goal which renders it meaningful.

Suppose, however, that we introduce the concept of our having *knowledge* of the eternal recurrence into our scenario. Such knowledge could, of course, effect no change in the recurrence. Nevertheless Nietzsche thought such knowledge might be liberating. If this life is your eternal life then what matters is what you eternally do.

---

[13] Charles Sanders Peirce, *Collected Papers*, ed. Charles Hartshorne and Paul Weiss (Cambridge, Mass.: Harvard University Press, 1935), 6.521.

The task is to give style to one's character and meaning to one's life to the extent that one can joyously affirm one's existence and welcome its eternal recurrence. This is, as it were, the optimistic perspective on eternal recurrence.

However the doctrine seems at least as plausibly to allow of a pessimistic perspective. The knowledge that we will have to endlessly repeat all that we have done could just as easily be experienced as crushing. The tedium of the picture is depressing. Just as a gesture repeated endlessly ceases to have the significance it originally did, so too with every episode in our lives until the ceaseless recurrence is felt to make every gesture senseless. Besides, there is a moral difficulty involved. Most lives include many wrong actions. The prospect of an infinite repetition of such wrong doings is distressing morally. Indeed, given the option of choosing such a recurrence, it may be that one is morally obliged to refuse it.

V

Perhaps these difficulties only arise with the eternal recurrence because each recurrence is an exact duplicate of the last. Consider instead, then, a series of disjoint lives such as is posited by Indian doctrines of rebirth. This does, of course, present some difficulties for the identity condition. For example, if memory is invoked as a sufficient condition of identity then we're back with the EM scenario and not with an alternative prospect. However let's suppose that these difficulties can be met. What, then, of the adequacy condition? Well at least EM's type of boredom can be avoided if we eliminate memory of past lives. Moreover, the possible variety of the disjoint lives presents an important disanalogy with the eternal recurrence scenario. Nevertheless the prospect of an infinite series of such lives ultimately may prove as nauseating as the prospect of eternal recurrence. Even allowing for considerable variety, human lives exhibit a number of characteristic general traits. And the prospect of this recurrence can just as easily be viewed pessimistically as the prospect of the eternal recurrence of this life.

Interestingly Bernard Williams seems to disagree here:

... I must confess that out of the alternatives it is the only one that for me
would, if it had sense, have any attraction — no doubt because it is the only
one which has the feature that what one is living at any given point is
actually *a life*. It is singular that those systems of belief that get closest to
actually accepting recurrence of this sort seem, almost without exception, to
look forward to the point when one will be released from it. Such systems
seem less interested in continuing one's life than in earning one the right to a
superior sort of death.[14]

Is it that this prospect (like that of eternal recurrence) seems also to admit of both
optimistic and pessimistic perspectives? What does the difference here consist in?

The difference between the optimist and the pessimist here is a difficult one to get
a handle on. Is it a disagreement about the facts? Not necessarily, suggests a well
known aphorism: "The optimist proclaims that we live in the best of all possible
worlds; and the pessimist fears that this is so." The point of this aphorism, of course, is
that both agree on the facts. In the terminology of the emotivists, what we seem to
have here is an agreement in belief but a difference in attitude. Is there any way to
break this deadlock? One way would be to try to change the beliefs of those involved.
But it seems possible that there could be agreement on these and yet disagreement on
the attitudes taken to the prospect of immortality. Of course judgements like "boring",
"painful" etc. are difficult to analyse here. Insofar as they are construed as hedonic
judgements they seem incorrigible. Disputes over whether the pleasures of eternal
existence would outweigh the disadvantages are disputes to which empirical beliefs are
obviously relevant. However the assertion "I find immortality enjoyable and hence it
is" seems more a straightforwardly incorrigible report about the immortal speaker's
hedonic states. It cannot be overturned by a rectificatory judgement of the form:
"Immortality is not enjoyable, though you mistakenly feel it to be so".

Now in the Indian context (to which, presumably, Williams is alluding) the
beginningless cycle of birth, death and rebirth (*saṃsāra*) is held to be inevitably characterized by *duḥkha* (suffering, sorrow). But it is also recognized that the ordinary

---

[14] Williams, pp. 93-94.

person, while not insensitive to the sorrows of life, generally feels that the transitory pleasures of life are sufficient in their intensity to compensate. This attitude of the worldling is considered by most Indian philosophers and religious thinkers to be one of the ordinary person's many ignorances. Indeed it is ignorance (*avidyā*) that keeps such a person caught in the vicious circle of *saṃsāra*. Clearly "*duḥkha*" is not simply a descriptive hedonic term, for then there could be no disputing the claim "I find *saṃsāra* enjoyable, hence it is so". Rather it is an evaluative term to be construed as more objective than a mere subjective feeling. Moreover *duḥkha* is not to be identified with pain, for pleasure (*sukha*) is widely acknowledged to be included in *duḥkha*. This is because worldly pleasure is inextricably entangled with pain, though not vice versa. (This point leads in turn to a disagreement among Indian philosophers as to whether liberation from the bondage of *saṃsāra* would involve some kind of eternal, positive pleasure. Thus the Nyāya, for example, holds liberation merely to involve absence of pain; whereas Advaita Vedānta maintains that the liberated soul experiences a positive bliss.)[15]

Empirical observations are, however, relevant to the claim "Life is *duḥkha*". Indeed close attention to the world is thought to bring this point home with particular force as we see how little our flickering joys alleviate the corresponding worries and dissatisfactions. But perhaps no entailment can be shown between such empirical observations and the judgement that all is *duḥkha*. However this in turn need not entail that is merely a subjective feeling, nor that the judgement "Life is *duḥkha*" is not a more appropriate response to the prospect of *saṃsāra* than the view of the hedonistic Cārvāka who mocks that all this would be as foolish as to give up rice because rice comes enfolded in husks.

VI

Some further interesting aspects of Indian thought can be highlighted by considering yet another scenario of immortality. Thus consider the possibility of an

---

[15] For an interesting discussion of this debate, based primarily on Nyāya materials, see A. Chakrabarti, "Is Liberation (*Mokṣa*) Pleasant?" *Philosophy East and West* 33 (1983): 167-182. On the concept of *duḥkha* see also Bimal Krishna Matilal, *Logical and Ethical Issues of Religious Belief* (Calcutta: University of Calcutta, 1982), Ch. 1.

eternal existence constantly improving in all ways. (This is a bit like the possibility envisaged in the Kantian argument for the postulate of immortality we discussed earlier,
but it also incorporates features from the other two arguments of that section.) This
scenario may not represent a necessary condition for value, but it might be claimed to
be a sufficient condition for value. However this claim too is unfounded. What makes
such a life valuable is not its eternal extension but the valuable qualities it exhibits.
Now the defender of this version of immortality will want to claim that the life's continuous improvement means that it would be a disvalue to end it at any point. And this
in turn seems to invite an Epicurean-style rejoinder that it cannot be a disvalue for the
person whose existence is ended because that the person is in existence is a presupposition of any claim that something is a disvalue (or value) for them. Of course, we have
already cast doubt upon the force of such an Epicurean argument. But perhaps what is
really being suggested here is that we accede to a Platonistic principle that it is better
for a (valuable) thing to exist than for it not to exist.[16] This, however, is to commit the
familiar error of treating existence as a perfection so that a thing is better for existing
than for not existing. It may, of course, be better for us (as existing beings) that a good
thing exist but the thing itself is no better for existing. Rather its existence is a
precondition of its having any value at all. As Gassendi put it, criticizing Descartes:

> But, sooth to say, existence is a perfection neither in God nor in anything
> else; it is rather that in the absence of which there is no perfection ... Hence
> neither is existence held to exist in a thing in that way that perfections do nor
> if the thing lacks existence is it said to be imperfect (or deprived of a
> perfection), so much as to be nothing.[17]

---

[16] I call this principle "Platonistic" since it seems to have an ancestral link with Plato's view that
Goodness itself is the source of both being and goodness in everything else (*Republic* 509). The
identity of being and goodness is certainly evident in Neo-Platonism: witness Plotinus' claim that the
One is both Being itself and the Good itself. Augustine takes over this view when he says that "every
entity, even if it is a defective one, in so far as it is an entity, is good" (*Enchiridion*, Ch. 13). The
principle that it is greater to exist in reality than not to do so is, of course, a presumption of Anselm's
first ontological argument (*Proslogion*, Ch. 2).

[17] *The Philosophical Works of Descartes*, Vol. 2, trans. E. S. Haldane and G. R. T. Ross (New
York: Dover, 1955), p. 186.

Now the metaphysics of Platonism and Neo-Platonism assert the identity of being and goodness and this doctrine was in turn incorporated into Christianity. But Platonism aside, no argument seems to be offered for the view that it is greater to exist in reality than not to do so. Of course, it is true that we do tend unreflectively to believe that it is better for us to exist in reality than in thought only. Indeed it might seem that otherwise we would have no reason to remain voluntarily in existence. But is this assumption justified? In the first place it is unclear what it is to compare the value of a real object with a merely imaginary object of the same description. One of two real objects may be better than the other, but how are real objects better or worse than imaginary ones? The Platonistic principle, however, requires such comparisons. But if we assume a Strawsonian account of referring here, then the truth-value of assertions of sentences of the form "The f is g" presupposes the existence of the entity the subject noun phrase refers to. If the subject of the sentence is only an imaginary object then, though the sentence is meaningful, the statement made in asserting that sentence is neither true nor false because one of its presuppositions is false. More particularly, assertions of sentences of a relational form require that the relational expression stand between two non-empty terms. For example, it cannot be true (or false) that I am taller than the present King of France. (Of course some philosophers wish to deny that value judgements have truth-values anyway and thus neither, on this account, will comparative value judgements. But presumably this position will hardly appeal to the Platonist.) Secondly, it does seem true that my desires can create interests which would be frustrated by my ceasing to exist and in this sense I can have a reason for voluntarily remaining in existence. But then it is the fulfilment of my interests that is the intrinsic value , not my continued existence.

This point in turn brings out another important Platonistic assumption about ultimate value that underpins a good deal of Christian theology and indeed much of Western thought: viz. that perfection is an intrinsic value, a good valued not for what it leads to but for what it is.[18] Given the doctrine of the identity of being and goodness, this seemed plausible. Indian thought, however, considers the quest for perfection to

---

[18] On perfectionism in Western thought see R. Newton Flew, *The Idea of Perfection in Christian Theology* (London: Oxford University Press, 1934); and John Passmore, *The Perfectibility of Man* (New York: Charles Scribner's Sons, 1970).

be the pursuit of an instrumental value. Perfection is valuable because it leads to the elimination of suffering (*duḥkha*) and it is the elimination of suffering that is intrinsically valuable, indeed the ultimate value. This is clearly implied by the structure of the Four Noble Truths in Buddhism. It is also apparent in philosophical Hinduism. Thus the *Sāṃkhyakārikā* begins: "Because of the torment of the threefold suffering arises the desire to know the means of removing it." And the *Nyāyasūtra* defines final release, the highest good (*niḥśreyasa*, literally "having no better") in terms of the complete absence of *duḥkha*. (Compare the Buddhist concept of *nirvāṇa*.) Thus to the question, "Why pursue the goal of perfection?" the Platonist has no answer other than, "Because it is intrinsically valuable." But Indian thinkers reply, "Because it leads to the elimination of suffering." This is a fundamental value difference between Western (Platonistic) thought and Indian thought. Moreover, the Indians also have a reply to the objection that if it is not better to exist in reality than merely in thought, then we can have no reason to remain voluntarily in existence. They hold that it is impossible to exit voluntarily from the circle of *saṃsāra* except by becoming a perfected being. The suicide is simply reborn in even more unfavourable circumstances.

With regard to the relative plausibility of claiming perfection or absence of suffering to be ultimate intrinsic values, the situation is rather more difficult. Consider, however, these two questions: (i) "Why do you want to be perfect?" and (ii) "Why do you want to eliminate suffering?" Now (ii) seems to be unanswerable in that anyone acting contrary to the general principle of eliminating suffering would seem irrational. Of course there might appear to be some counterexamples. The masochist, for instance, seeks suffering; but that is because it provides a greater pleasure. The saint ignores his own suffering; but that is in favour of eliminating the suffering of others. Altruism is perfectly consistent with taking the elimination of suffering generally to be an intrinsic value. Consider (i) however. Fania Pascal recalls a conversation with Wittgenstein:

> At one stage I cried out: "What is it? You want to be perfect?" And he pulled himself up proudly, saying: "Of *course* I want to be perfect".[19]

---

[19] "Wittgenstein: A Personal Memoir" in C. G. Luckhardt, ed., *Wittgenstein: Sources and Perspectives* (Hassocks: Harvester Press, 1979), p. 48.

The anecdote has piquancy precisely because the "Of *course*" is not trivial. What makes Wittgenstein's reply so revealing of his character is that this goal seemed so *obviously* the right one to him. Nevertheless it certainly does not seem irrational to set oneself a different goal in the way that denying the goal of eliminating suffering seems irrational. Now this feature does not show that perfection is not an intrinsic value — we could admit a plurality of intrinsic values. But it does lend plausibility to the suggestion that perfection is a less *basic* intrinsic value than elimination of suffering. Anyway, given that the elimination of suffering is a basic intrinsic value in this way and given also some not unreasonable empirical observations about the nature of the world, the Indians do not generally consider personal immortality to be of value. (Unless, of course, it is instrumentally valuable in eliminating the suffering of others: consider the *bodhisattva* ideal in Mahāyāna Buddhism.)

VII

One final scenario. It might be thought that my discussion so far is deficient in an important respect. I have taken "immortality" to mean endless temporal duration, whereas it should be understood to mean *timelessness*. This interpretation chimes in with the Christian theological tradition that holds God to be a timeless being. Now the theological doctrine of God's timelessness was held by a number of influential figures including Augustine, Boethius and Aquinas — though whether the theist is wise to adopt such a view of God is dubious. [20] However it is clear that the notion of timeless post-mortem existence won't help make the doctrine of immortality any more attractive. Indeed immortality thus understood would fail to satisfy both the identity and the adequacy conditions.

The identity condition will not be satisfied because a timeless being will not clearly be *me*. A timeless being could not deliberate and reflect since these mental acts take time, i.e. they require that the agent have temporal *extension*. Nor could a timeless being anticipate or intend, since these activities require that the agent have

---

[20] A good discussion of this question is to be found in Nelson Pike, *God and Timelessness* (London: Routledge & Kegan Paul, 1970).

temporal *position* relative to what is anticipated or intended. Nor could a timeless being remember, since such a being cannot have a past. Thus there is a large class of actions that a timeless being must be incapable of. Indeed this class of actions is so large that it is unclear that such a being could even be counted as a *person* at all. But even if such a being were marginally to count as a person, just how much of a person would he be? This question impinges on both the identity and adequacy conditions. Firstly, even if the timeless being is a person, is he enough of a person to be *me*? Secondly, even if the timeless person is me, would such a circumscribed mode of existence be valuable? With regard to this latter question we have good reason for negative expectations. Not only would the timeless being be incapable of a huge range of actions, but such a being would be totally immutable. Indeed the logical connection between total immutability and timelessness seems to have been a major theological motive for the claim that God is timeless. Hence Aquinas held that "something lacking change and never varying its mode of existence will not display a before and after" (*Summa Theologiae* Ia, 10, 1). Thus God's timelessness supposedly "follows upon unchangeableness, and God alone ... is altogether unchangeable" (Ia, 10, 3). Aquinas, however, mistook the entailment relation involved between the two doctrines and erroneously held that God's immutability entailed His timelessness, whereas it is God's alleged timelessness that would entail His immutability. But the important point for our purposes here is that the situation of the timeless and hence immutable "person" is the EM scenario *par excellence*, a scenario that cannot satisfy the adequacy condition.

Finally, it is by no means obvious that the doctrine of timelessness can even be coherently expressed. This is trenchantly brought out in Wittgenstein's remark:

> Philosophers who say: "after death a timeless state will begin", or: "at death a timeless state begins", and do not notice that they have used the words "after" and "at" and "begins" in a temporal sense, and that temporality is embedded in their grammar.[21]

---

[21] Ludwig Wittgenstein, *Culture and Value* (Oxford: Basil Blackwell, 1980), p. 22 e.

VIII

To sum up then. Our first three scenarios each represent a version of immortality, but none of these versions is an attractive one. The fourth scenario is not so much unattractive as insufficient for value. The fifth (timeless) scenario satisfies neither the identity condition nor the adequacy condition. Hence even if a normal life has value for me, this does not entail that the infinite extension or repetition of it would. None of these versions of immortality is sufficient to guarantee the meaningfulness of a life. This has, of course, been recognized by some writers. Theists, for example, typically expect a transformed quality of life in the hereafter. But then there is no reason why a life cannot now instance this transformed quality and hence have eternal value. In this spirit Tolstoy insists in his *What I Believe* that "eternal life" refers to a quality of life *now*. The fear of death is the response to the realization that one's life does not possess this quality and death will destroy its meaning. This line of argument is interestingly developed in D. Z. Phillips' *Death and Immortality*:

> Eternity is not an extension of this present life, but a mode of judging it. Eternity is not more life, but this life seen under certain moral and religious modes of thought.[22]

Immortality is the turning towards these moral attitudes, "living and dying in a way which could not be rendered pointless by death" (p. 50).

With regard to the adequacy of this sort of account, two separate questions need to be distinguished: (i) "Is this sense of 'eternal life' sufficient to guarantee the meaningfulness of a life?" and (ii) "Is this sort of account adequate to the traditional religious view of immortality?" In answer to (i) it seems to me that it is. In answer to (ii) the matter is more complex. Accounts like Phillips' are frequently castigated as

---

[22] D. Z. Phillips, *Death and Immortality* (London: Macmillan, 1970), p. 49. Phillips' account here has been influenced by similar suggestions presented in Stewart R. Sutherland, "Immortality and Resurrection" *Religious Studies* 3 (1968): 377-389; and "'What Happens After Death?'" *Scottish Journal of Theology* 22 (1969): 404-418. (Compare also Wittgenstein's *Tractatus* 6.4312.)

"reductionist".[23] About this charge I just want to make two points. First, the reductionist charge is always a delicate one to handle. After all (to take but one example), few modern Christian theologians believe all the dogmas that their predecessors did. What is central to a system of religious beliefs and what is not is very difficult to determine. It is prudent to be chary of labelling new interpretations of traditional concepts "reductionist" if we mean by this "inadequate".[24] Secondly, even if Phillips' account is inadequate to traditional Christian understanding of immortality it is necessary to recall the context of his argument. Preliminary to the chapters in *Death and Immortality* that present this account is a critique of traditional views about disembodied existence and resurrection. If Phillips is correct in believing these views to be philosophically incoherent, then the only viable sense of "eternal life" must be one like that he gives it. But to show this, of course, requires that traditional conceptions like disembodied existence, resurrection and rebirth are indeed untenable. And this in turn requires detailed investigation and argument ...

---

[23] See, for example, Patrick Sherry, *Religion, Truth and Language-Games* (London: Macmillan, 1977).

[24] On this point compare J. C. Thornton, "Religious Belief and 'Reductionism'" *Sophia* 5 (3) (1966): 3-16.

CHAPTER 6: DISEMBODIED EXISTENCE

I

One traditional conception of immortality involves the notion that we survive death in a disembodied form. In Western thought this is familiar as the doctrine of the immortality of the soul. This doctrine (which entered Christianity from Greek philosophy) is one of the two major versions of immortality presented in the Western Christian tradition; the other, of course, is the doctrine of the resurrection of the body. Whether these two versions of immortality are compatible, or (supposing that they are incompatible) which of these two versions is the more authentically Christian one, are matters that need not concern us here.[1] Rather, what I shall be concerned with is the philosophical credibility of the notion of disembodied existence.

An immediate difficulty that arises for many confronting the possibility of disembodied existence is that it requires (if it is to be more than a mere logical possibility) that some form of mind-body dualism be true. Recent work in analytical philosophy of mind has been inimical to dualism. Indeed various forms of materialism have dominated the philosophical scene in recent years. But if the doctrine of disembodied post-mortem existence is true, materialism must be false. Now I don't want to enter into the difficulties of the mind-body problem here. Rather all I shall do is note that disembodied existence is logically tied to dualism in this way, a link that renders the doctrine itself highly implausible to many contemporary philosophers. However it is worth noting that while disembodied existence implies dualism, dualism does not entail disembodied existence. This is an important point for even if dualism is true, this need not mean that the doctrine of disembodied existence is true. Indeed the dualist espousal of this doctrine may well seem anomolous. After all, the sophisticated

---

[1] On these matters compare Oscar Cullman, *Immortality of the Soul or Resurrection of the Dead?* (London: Epworth, 1958). For criticism of Cullman's views see H. A. Wolfson, *Religious Philosophy* (Cambridge, Mass.: Harvard University Press, 1961), Ch. 3; and George W. E. Nickelsburg, Jr, *Resurrection, Immortality, and Eternal Life in Intertestamental Judaism* (Cambridge, Mass.: Harvard University Press, 1972), pp. 177-180.

modern dualist is well aware of the innumerable concomitances between physical and mental changes that the biological sciences have detailed for us. But having conceded these innumerable causal interactions between the mental and the physical, the dualist committed to disembodied existence wants to assert that these causal interactions come to an end at death and the mind lives on. There is no contradiction in saying this, of course, as there would be if a materialist were to claim that minds survive the dissolution of brains. However it is nevertheless odd.

The point at issue here is well made by Hume:

> Where any two objects are so closely connected that all alterations which we have ever seen in the one are attended with proportionable alterations in the other; we ought to conclude, by all rules of analogy, that, when there are still greater alterations produced in the former, and it is totally dissolved, there follows a total dissolution of the latter ... The weakness of the body and that of the mind in infancy are exactly proportioned; their vigour in manhood, their sympathetic disorder in sickness, their common gradual decay in old age. The step further seems unavoidable; their common dissolution in death.[2]

As with most analogical reasoning, the argument is inconclusive. Compare in this regard Ewing's counterargument for the defence:

> ... to argue that because under present conditions we cannot think without the brain, we shall be unable to think when we have no brain might be like arguing that, because I cannot see the sky in my study without looking through the window, I shall be unable to see it when I have gone out of the house because I shall have no windows to look through.[3]

---

[2] "On the Immortality of the Soul" in Richard Wollheim, ed., *Hume on Religion* (London: Fontana, 1963), pp. 267-268.

[3] A. C. Ewing, *Non-Linguistic Philosophy* (London: George Allen & Unwin, 1968), p. 172. Ewing is self-avowedly indebted to the original simile in J. M. E. McTaggart, *Some Dogmas of Religion* , p. 105.

It remains possible, then, that the mind, though in continuous interaction with the brain throughout mortal life, should nevertheless survive the death of the body. That is, that the mind should be immortal though the brain is mortal. However, it is surely somewhat odd to assert this. But then the dualist committed to disembodied existence will want to say that it is at least as odd to admit the ontological independence of mind and body and yet deny that the former might survive the extinction of the latter. Perhaps each possibility is intuitively as plausible (or implausible) as the other. Anyway, it does at least seem that the impasse here will presumably only be resolved by appeal to philosophical considerations other than just the mind-body question. And, of course, it is these other beliefs that will render one or the other of the two possibilities more or less plausible to a particular person.[4]

II

But even if we put aside these questions that attend dualism there still remain philosophical difficulties with the doctrine of disembodied post-mortem existence. These difficulties cluster around two points. First, what sort of "survival" of death would be involved in disembodied existence, given the attenuation of person-predicates appropriate to such a mode of existence? Secondly, what sense can be attached to the claim that such a disembodied being is the *same* person as the ante-mortem embodied being? In other words, is a disembodied mind a *person*; and, if it is a person, is it the *same* person as the ante-mortem person?[5] Let us attend to these questions in more detail.

In the first place the class of person-predicates ascribable to disembodied persons seems a severely reduced class when compared with the class of person-predicates ascribable to embodied persons. For example, disembodied persons cannot walk, talk, touch things, etc. However perhaps they can still be said to perceive and to act if we

---

[4] Of course, some dualists are sensitive to this impasse. See, for example, John Hick, *Death and Eternal Life* , p. 126; and Paul and Linda Badham, *Immortality or Extinction?* (London: Macmillan, 1982), pp. 39-41.

[5] For an elegant and influential treatment of these questions see Terence Penelhum, *Survival and Disembodied Existence* (London: Routledge & Kegan Paul, 1970).

understand these terms in a suitably attenuated sense. Thus "perceive" will imply no more than having perceptual-type experiences. Taking the case of "seeing", this will mean having a set of visual images similar phenomenologically to the sort of images a perceiver would have if the perceptual object were there. Similarly "hearing" and "feeling" would involve only corresponding auditory and tactile experiences. In the case of "acting" it seems that there are certain difficulties with the notion of disembodied agency. Hence if disembodied agents are going to be allowed to act upon the physical world such actions will have to be basic actions, i.e. actions the performance of which does not require other actions to be done in order to perform those actions. But disembodied beings can apparently act in some sense.

Nevertheless such a mode of existence will seem to many not merely a very thin and unattractive one, but incoherent as a version of immortality. That is, it will be objected that, while such disembodied beings may be possible, they would not be fully *persons* and hence cannot represent survival in any personally interesting sense. It must be *me* that survives, not some fragment of me. However it is unclear that this objection is sound, for H. H. Price has presented an ingenious scenario of disembodied existence that suggests the prospect is both intelligible and potentially interesting personally.[6]

Price suggests that the world of disembodied beings would be a kind of dream-world. In dreams we are deprived of sensory stimuli and yet sometimes have very vivid and exciting experiences. Similarly, life after death would be a kind of dream from which we would not awake but in which we would nevertheless retain our memories, desires and characters. Hence death would be a change of consciousness analogous to what happens in ante-mortem life when we fall asleep and begin to dream. Now dream images have spatial properties (at least relative to each other), though they are unlocated in physical space. Hence the dream-world created by memory would resemble the physical world, except the causal laws would be different. For instance, if a disembodied person desired to be in a certain place, he

---

[6] H. H. Price, "Survival and the Idea of 'Another World'" in Terence Penelhum, ed., *Immortality* (Belmont, Calif.: Wadsworth, 1973), pp. 21-47; and *Essays in the Philosophy of Religion* (Oxford: Clarendon Press, 1972), Ch. 6.

instantaneously would find himself there, without any intermediate passage. This sort of phenomenon would enable him to infer that he was no longer in the physical world.

The subjective quality of these image-worlds seem to threaten an after-life of (epistemic) solipsism. But Price replies that this is not necessarily so. Although there would need to be many Next Worlds, it is possible that telepathic communications could take place so that there might be a common image-world that is jointly produced by several telepathically interacting disembodied persons. (In this regard Price mentions the evidence for telepathic dreams and communications presented by psychical researchers.) These common dream-worlds would link only like-minded personalities so that each group of like-minded personalities would have a different Next World, public to members of the group but private to the group as a whole. This feature makes room for certain eschatological teachings in many religious traditions. (Recall here Jesus' saying (John 14:2): "In my Father's house are many mansions ...")

However Price still thinks that the picture sketched so far is insufficient as it stands. A person needs a body to be a *social* being, and a being incapable of social relations would not be a *person*. There are two reasons why a social being requires a body. First, to express her mental states in an overt and perceptible manner. In order to be a person you must have, for instance, a face which others can respond to. Second, to enter into social relations of any significant kind a person must be recognizable. Thus personal existence apparently requires some form of embodiment. In order to meet this requirement without postulating an actual physical body (and hence abandoning the notion of disembodied existence), Price posits an image-body. This would be a public, spatial entity (though, as with dream images, not located in physical space). This last postulate leads Price to suggest that after all the disembodied conception of survival may not be as sharply contrasted with the embodied conception as it might at first appear. In effect the two conceptions seem to converge.

Of course, it remains to be argued that this conception of disembodied existence is actually instantiated. However it does seem that the scenario (the ingenious details of which I have no space to discuss here), is a coherent and worthwhile one. Indeed it is interesting to note that Price remarks:

You may have noticed that the Next World, according to my account of it, is not at all unlike what some metaphysicians say *this* world is ... Could it be that these Idealist metaphysicians have given us a substantially correct picture of the next world, though a mistaken picture of this one?[7]

Now the long history of philosophical controversy concerning the truth of idealism surely suggests that while idealism may be a false account of our world, it is by no means clear that it is an incoherent view, nor a view that if true would be irrelevant personally. Thus if the analogy holds, Price has succeeded in presenting an intelligible account of what existence as a disembodied person might be like.

III

But even if Price's scenario of disembodied existence is a coherent one there still remains a further problem. Given that we can make sense of the notion of disembodied persons, what grounds could we have for identifying these disembodied beings as being the *same* persons as particular deceased persons? This is the second of the two major difficulties with the doctrine of disembodied existence, i.e. the identity problem. And in fact this is the problem that has most concerned recent philosophers. The difficulty here is how to justify a claim that the disembodied person is the same person as the dead person. Two criteria of personal identity have commonly been offered. One is the bodily criterion that makes the identity of persons dependent on the identity of the bodies they have. The other is the memory criterion that makes the identity of person A with person B depend upon A's having memories of the experiences of B. Of course in our ordinary ascriptions of personal identity we often use both of these criteria. However, whether one of these two criteria is prior to the other is of considerable significance for the credibility of disembodied survival of death. Hence if bodily identity is a necessary condition of personal identity, then it is obvious that we cannot survive death as disembodied persons. Even if there could exist such disembodied beings, in the absence of a body no disembodied being could be

---

7 "Survival and the Idea of 'Another World'", p. 46.

identified as the *same person* as any ante-mortem person. Furthermore, if bodily identity is necessary for personal identity then the whole notion of a bodiless individual is problematic. How does this bodiless individual maintain its own identity through time?

Thus the defender of the doctrine of disembodied survival will be tempted to opt for the memory criterion of identity. But the difficulty here is that we need to distinguish between *really* remembering and *seeming* to remember. Clearly, apparent memories cannot provide a criterion of personal identity, for otherwise I could "remember" events that never occurred and be identical with someone who never existed. However if we proffer *real* memories as the criterion of identity then we are in effect saying that A is the same person as B if (i) the experiences that A claims to remember occurring to B actually occurred to B; and (ii) these experiences actually occurred to A (i.e. A is the same person as B). But the addition of this second requirement makes the condition circular. A can only *actually* remember being B if A *is B*, which is what A's "memories" of being B are being invoked to settle. Thus since the memory condition presupposes personal identity, such identity cannot itself rest upon memory.[8] But then it seems natural to revert to the criterion of bodily identity and with it a correspondingly negative appraisal of the possibility of disembodied post-mortem existence.

There is a certain irony in the way the identity problem bedevils the notion of disembodied survival. After all, the idea of disembodied survival is most familiar as the doctrine of the immortality of the soul. And part of the appeal of positing souls in the first place is that they seem to promise a solution to the problem of personal identity. In other words, it is suggested that there is some constituent of a person which remains constant as he or she undergoes physical and psychical change and it is this constituent (call it "the soul") which we are identifying when we identify someone as the same person. Queries about who a person really is are thus translatable into queries about which soul is linked with a designated body. The soul remains identical while the body, and even the personality, change in the course of time. If the soul is the

---

[8] This important point was first made in the eighteenth century by Bishop Butler in his "Of Personal Identity": see *The Works of Joseph Butler*, Vol. 1, ed. W. E. Gladstone (Oxford: Clarendon Press, 1896), p. 388.

same soul at two given times, then the person is the same person. If the souls are different, then we have different persons.

This account might seem to have a prima facie appeal as a lucid solution to the problem of personal identity. However, upon analysis the position turns out to be rife with difficulties.[9] The central question involved is: "What is meant by a soul being the same or different?" Two possible answers readily present themselves. First, that a soul can change in whatever ways souls do but still remain the same soul. Second, any change in a soul makes it a different soul. Both replies involve us in incoherencies.

If we take up the first answer and maintain that possibly a soul might change its characteristics and yet remain the same soul, then it is also at least possible that a soul's characteristics be similar to a person's. Thus as I change my tastes so does my soul. This now enables us to identify a given soul by reference to its characteristics but simultaneously eliminates the criterion of personal identity that was being offered for cases where someone's tastes, personality etc. changed radically over a period of time and yet we still wanted to call them the same person. The whole appeal of souls in the problem of personal identity rests on their apparent utility in establishing that somebody is the same person if he or she has the same soul. If souls change as people change, then what is our criterion for a soul being the same when it has itself changed radically? A super-soul? And then, of course, we are into a regress.

Suppose instead, then, that we take up the second answer to our original question about the identity of souls and maintain that a change in a soul makes it a different soul. Now we will have to admit that if somebody can alter considerably yet remain the same person because he or she has the same soul, then a soul's characteristics can only be very loosely connected with a person's. We seem to have two choices about what to hold here. First, we could argue that a soul's characteristics are typologically related to a person's, but cannot be directly inferred from a person's. Second, we could argue that a soul's characteristics are of an entirely different sort and not knowable in the manner in which we usually come to know somebody.

---

[9] Cf. the discussion (to which I am indebted here) in J. F. M. Hunter, *Essays After Wittgenstein* (Toronto: University of Toronto, 1973), pp. 33-36. Some of this argumentation is prefigured in John Locke, *An Essay Concerning Human Understanding*, Bk. 2, Ch. 27.

If we pursue the latter argument then we are in the unhappy position of having to invent or discover characteristics hitherto unknown to humankind. Prior to this achievement only God would know who anyone really was. Furthermore, since we do not already know how to settle questions of identity prior to this discovery, then how can we decide whether these new characteristics are really identifying characteristics and not merely newly discovered properties of persons which can change radically without affecting the ascription of personal identity? Even if we discovered some un-alterable characteristic of a person during his or her life, we would still need to show (i) that an instance of this property can adequately characterize a particular individual; and (ii) that an alteration or elimination of this property would entail that someone was a *different* person (rather than no longer a person).

On the other hand, if we pursue the first line of argument suggested above and assert that souls have characteristics only typologically related to persons, then the difficulty is how to justify ascribing such characteristics to the soul. Any property attributed as an identifying characteristic could just as easily be a hitherto undiscovered accidental attribute.

Hence the soul theory of identity faces formidable difficulties. The nub of the theory is the apparently plausible view that when we identify somebody as the same person what we are identifying (or at least presuming the continued existence of) is a constant *X* that has remained the same while other things have (or have not) altered. But any theory of this type faces the same problem. On the one hand, no matter what this constant *X* is, it must possess individuating characteristics in order for its presence to be able to show who a person is (though at most only that he or she is human). On the other hand, it cannot be the case that this *X* possesses any of the characteristics by which we identify humans, for it is agreed that these characteristics can alter radically without our necessarily declaring someone no longer to be the same man or woman.

The vacuity of the soul theory as a solution to the problem of personal identity should thus make it unsurprising to us that the notion of disembodied survival faces an identity problem. And this difficulty about the memory criterion presupposing personal identity will not be met by appeal to the notion of the soul as a changeless substance in which psychical changes inhere. In the first place we have once again a concept empirically useless for our epistemic difficulties about identifying persons. Secondly, there is a deeper disquietude about the whole notion of a spiritual substance which cannot be independently characterized apart from the insistence that it is this entity that provides the identity-guaranteeing condition. As Penelhum puts it:

> Beyond the wholly empty assurance that it is a metaphysical principle which guarantees continuing identity through time, or the argument that since we know identity persists some such principle must hold in default of others, no content seems available for the doctrine ... [The] doctrine amounts to no more than a pious assurance that all is well, deep down. It provides no reason for this assurance.[10]

IV

How, then, can we respond to this difficulty about the identity of disembodied persons? I want to mention two possibilities.[11] The first is a suggestion offered by Peter Geach, who in turn derives it from Aquinas.[12] Now Geach is not very sanguine about the intelligibility of ascribing sensations and feelings to a disembodied spirit anyway. Of course, (as he admits) this does not mean that there cannot be such spirits. However if my soul is such a spirit, then even if my soul survives my death, this need not mean that *I* do. But Geach also has another worry about disembodied survival, viz.

---

[10] Penelhum, *Survival and Disembodied Existence*, pp. 76-77.

[11] There is a third possibility that I do not intend to treat of in any detail. Perhaps the most vigorous contemporary advocate of this view is Hywel D. Lewis: see particularly his *The Self and Immortality* (London: Macmillan, 1973); *Persons and Life After Death* (London: Macmillan, 1978); and *The Elusive Self* (London: Macmillan, 1982). The approach basically consists in the claim that, not only are there substantial selves distinct from our experiences, characters, memories and dispositions, but that we are quite simply and directly aware of ourselves as such *sui generis* entities. That is, I am supposed simply to recognize my self as the particular continuing entity I happen to find myself to be. In response to this I would deny that we all have this experience of the self (unless the trivial sense in which I am directly aware that I am me is all that is meant). Furthermore, I would also maintain that even if we did have such intuitions about the self, our theories are not necessarily obliged to do justice to such intuitive realism (as I have already argued in Chapter 2).

[12] Peter Geach, *God and the Soul* (London: Routledge & Kegan Paul, 1969), Ch. 2

the identity problem. For even if such dehumanized thought is possible, just *whose* thought would it be? How could there be *one* or *many* disembodied minds to think these thoughts? With no criterion of identity whereby we can distinguish one disembodied mind from another, we correspondingly have no surviving individuality in the sense required to make intelligible the claim that *I* might survive *my* death. Attempts to differentiate two disembodied minds in terms of differences in memories and aims must fail, for such differences presuppose that the two minds are already distinct.

Well perhaps we could say that two disembodied minds are distinct in respect of being the souls of different bodies and remain so differentiated when no longer embodied. This is essentially Geach's line, but with an important qualification:

> I do not think this solution would do at all if differentiation by reference to different bodies were merely retrospective. It might be otherwise if we held, with Aquinas, that the relation to a body was not merely retrospective — that each disembodied human soul permanently retained a capacity for reunion to such a body as would reconstitute a man identifiable with the man who died. This might satisfactorily account for the individuation of disembodied human souls; they would differ by being fitted for reunion to different bodies; but it would entail that the possibility of disembodied human souls stood or fell with the *possibility* of a dead man's living again *as a man*.[13]

It is unclear, however, that this move will really vindicate disembodied survival. In the first place disembodied survival on this account must be a temporary state. Otherwise we will have to believe that a disembodied soul

> ... whose very identity depends on the capacity for reunion with one human body rather than another, will continue to exist for ever with this capacity unrealized.[14]

---

[13] Ibid., p. 23.
[14] Ibid., p. 28.

In other words, the real possibilities for immortality are resurrection or (perhaps) reincarnation — though Geach himself is hostile to the latter.[15] In any case, disembodied existence does not represent a genuine scenario for *immortality*.

Secondly, on this account the identity problem about disembodied survival is to be resolved by reference to a future resurrection (or reincarnation). But though the resurrected persons will have bodies and hence admit of differentiation in terms of bodily criteria like spatio-temporal location, the question will still arise as to the identity of these resurrected persons with the deceased persons they resemble. Are they the *same* persons as the dead persons, or are they duplicates? There are various ways to try to deal with this query. One way is to admit that there is a gap between the ante-mortem life and the post-mortem resurrection life. Persons, it is then argued, are gap-inclusive entities (like wars or performances of plays) and the resurrectee can be most conveniently described as the same person as the deceased. This account of resurrection is logically quite distinct from the doctrine of the immortality of the soul. Indeed this type of answer makes no appeal to the notion of disembodied post-mortem existence at all. But if the soul is going to drop out of the picture altogether, there seems little point in worrying about identity criteria for disembodied souls in the first place.

A different approach is to insist that in spite of the time gap between the death and the appearance of the resurrected body, something persists in between and it is this that provides for identity. It is here that the disembodied soul might be invoked as the intermediate bearer of identity. But this is clearly unsatisfactory. The original problem was to provide a criterion of identity for such disembodied souls. Geach's suggestion was that this could be done by reference to future resurrection bodies. But what makes a resurrectee identical with a deceased person? To appeal to the intermediate existence of a disembodied soul will be patently circular if the identity of the soul is in turn to be dependent on a "capacity for reunion to such a body as would reconstitute a man identifiable with the man who died."[16]

---

[15] Ibid., Ch. 1.

[16] Ibid., p. 23.

The second possible response to the identity problem about disembodied existence is more radical. Penelhum alludes to it briefly in discussing the problem of distinguishing one object of reference or address *from others*:

Clearly no incorporeal being can be so distinguished, not just because he cannot be seen or *picked out*, but because in the absence of any body we cannot give content to the individuation of one such being from another, just as we cannot give content to the notion of some mental act being performed by the same incorporeal being who performed a previous one, rather than by another. But perhaps this only shows that it is incoherent (as indeed it is) to hold there could be a *plurality* of incorporeal beings. It might be possible to hold not that there cannot be any, but that there must either be none, or only one.[17]

One way to interpret this suggestion is that disembodied survival may be possible for one person but one person only. The interest of such a claim will then depend upon who that one person is and what relation he or she has to the person contemplating this possibility. However Penelhum is presumably hinting at a more radical prospect than this: some version, perhaps, of a monistic eschatology which holds that upon death we are absorbed into a single all-embracing disembodied spirit. Of course, our sense of personal distinctiveness will be lost. But such an eschatology provides for disembodied immortality of a sort, even if it isn't strictly speaking *personal* immortality. In the West views like this have been held by various monistic philosophers like Plotinus and (with certain qualifications) Spinoza, and also by some Christian mystics like (perhaps) Meister Eckhart. But in general the view has been a minority option in the West both because the monism implicitly contradicts the orthodox Christian insistence on a sharp dualism between God and His creation, and also because the "survival" offered is too thin a notion to be humanly interesting to most. In India, however, such a view represents an important strand within Hinduism, the most influential and systematic treatment of which is to be found in the non-dualist philosophical school of Advaita Vedānta. Within the Hindu tradition, then, such a monistic eschatology is a

---

[17] Penelhum, *Survival and Disembodied Existence*, p. 108. Compare also the concluding remarks in his "Survival and Identity: Some Recent Discussions" in Mostafa Faghfoury, ed., *Analytical Philosophy of Religion in Canada* (Ottawa: University of Ottawa, 1982), pp. 35-53.

major and living option and so it is instructive to examine some of the philosophical discussion about this view within Hinduism.

V

In order to understand properly the Hindu eschatology presented in Advaita Vedānta a couple of preliminary points are necessary. Firstly, that the monistic picture under discussion is a particular Hindu *eschatology*, rather than a "paraeschatology".[18] That is, it is a picture of the ultimate post-mortem state (*mokṣa*), rather than a picture of what happens between death and that ultimate state. In Advaita Vedānta (as in all Hindu thought) it is held that ordinary beings after death are reincarnated again. Only those who have freed themselves of binding ignorance (*avidyā*) will achieve the final state of release (*mokṣa*) wherein human individuality has been left behind. Secondly, although this monistic picture is evident in various of the *Upaniṣads* (and hence scripturally based), Advaita Vedānta is only *one* Hindu philosophical system. It has been (and remains) one of the most important and influential Hindu views, but it would nevertheless be an error to mistake it for *the* Hindu position. Within Vedānta alone there are rival schools like Viśiṣṭādvaita and Dvaita that oppose Advaitin monism in the cause of theism. Similarly, both Vaiṣṇava theologians (like Nimbārka and the followers of Caitanya) and the school of Śaiva Siddhānta insist on a dualism between God and His creation. Finally, within the orthodox six schools of Hindu philosophy (*ṣaḍ-darśana*) Nyāya, Vaiśeṣika, Sāṃkhya, Yoga and Mīmāṃsā all affirm that *mokṣa* involves the existence of innumerable, monadic disembodied selves.

A good example of this latter view can be found in what is probably the oldest of the Indian dualist schools: viz. Sāṃkhya, classically expounded in Īśvarakṛṣṇa's *Sāṃkhyakārikā*.[19] Indeed, in order to understand the Advaitin position better it will be

---

[18] This useful terminology was coined by John Hick in his *Death and Eternal Life*, p. 12.

[19] For translations of this and other Sāṃkhya texts see Sarvepalli Radhakrishnan and Charles A. Moore, eds., *A Sourcebook in Indian Philosophy* (Princeton: Princeton University Press, 1957), p. 426-452. A useful secondary work on Sāṃkhya is Gerald J. Larson, *Classical Sāṃkhya* 2nd rev. ed. (Delhi: Motilal Banarsidass, 1979) which includes both a review of the interpretative literature, and the Sanskrit text of the *Kārikās* together with an English translation.

helpful, first, to say a little about the Sāṃkhya system; and, secondly, to indicate how Advaita can be seen as developing some of its characteristic theses in relation to difficulties implicit in the Sāṃkhya view.

Sāṃkhya is clearly a dualistic system in that it espouses a radical division of reality into two categories: *puruṣa* ("spirit", "soul") and *prakṛti* ("nature", "matter"). Suffering is caused by our confusion of *puruṣa* with *prakṛti* and emancipation follows from correct understanding of the real nature of *puruṣa* and its difference from *prakṛti*. In keeping with its intellectualistic conception of liberation, Sāṃkhya attempts to present rational *arguments* for its major theses. Thus the existence of *puruṣa* is argued for (*Kārikā* XVII) on the grounds that consciousness exists and distinctions in the world are *for* this consciousness which is itself apart from the world. If it were not so apart *puruṣa* would be determined by the world and liberation would be impossible. Moreover there must be a plurality of *puruṣas* because otherwise whatever happens to one consciousness will happen at the same time to every consciousness, which is contrary to the perceived diversity of births, deaths and faculties (XVIII).

Prakṛti, on the other hand, is a unitary material substance which evolves into the world we perceive through our senses. The proximity of *puruṣa* acts as a catalyst in releasing the causal transformation of primordial nature (*mūlaprakṛti*) into the whole of the perceptible world (XX). It is important to note, however, that while Sāṃkhya insists on a dualism of *puruṣa* and *prakṛti*, the intellect (*buddhi*) is itself considered to be a highly refined type of matter. Hence there is no mind-body dualism here as in Western metaphysics, for while *puruṣa* is individual consciousness, it is itself inactive. The active, personal self-consciousness in Sāṃkhya is associated with the notions of *buddhi*, *ahaṃkāra* and *manas*, i.e. the first evolutes of *prakṛti*.

Now Sāṃkhya maintains that the association of *puruṣa* and *prakṛti* is the cause of suffering. Thus it is held to be crucial to recognize that *puruṣa* and *prakṛti* are absolutely separate. *Puruṣa* is not in fact bound to the world but merely appears so to the undiscriminating. Rather only *prakṛti* in its various forms transmigrates, is bound and is released (LXII). Even though *puruṣa* and *prakṛti* are in proximity to and association with each other and this proximity activates the evolution of *prakṛti*, they remain nonetheless entirely separate realities. The soteriological goal is *kaivalya* (literally "isolation") wherein the true nature of the *puruṣa* as "pure consciousness" is rediscovered. Sāṃkhya eschatology offers a picture of innumerable monadic *puruṣas* in *kaivalya*.

Two points are especially worth noting about this picture. Firstly, the "pure consciousness" gambit might be seen as an attempt to meet the difficulties mentioned earlier that attend the ascription of feelings and sensations to disembodied souls. The *puruṣa* is just pure, contentless consciousness; its condition in *kaivalya* is a condition in which consciousness is no longer consciousness of something. However this leads us to the second point. Even if *puruṣas* are not personal, they are supposed to be individual and a plurality of them is supposed to exist. But, as the Advaitins were quick to point out, there is no sense in talking of a plurality of pure, contentless consciousnesses. What distinguishes one consciousness from another? Thus, while Advaita accepts the intelligibility of the notion of a pure, contentless consciousness, it insists that there can only be *one* such consciousness, i.e. *Brahman*. The crux of Advaita is the assertion of non-duality between the Self (*ātman*) and the Absolute (*Brahman*). Advaita interprets the Upaniṣadic "*tat tvam asi*" ("Thou art that") to mean that *Brahman* and *ātman* are in reality one. The highest truth (*paramārtha*) is that there exists only one supreme contentless consciousness, although in terms of our ordinary (*vyāvahārika*) knowledge it is proper to talk of individual transmigrating selves (*jīvas*).

This position is by no means free of difficulties. Some of these centre around the notion of a pure, contentless consciousness. In his *Śrībhāṣya* (I.1.1) the Viśiṣṭādvaitin philosopher Rāmānuja puts forward some trenchant criticisms of this notion. Firstly, Rāmānuja argues that consciousness is irreducibly intentional: it is always *someone's* consciousness of *something*. Here he appeals to ordinary usage:

... as appears from ordinary judgments such as "I know the jar", "I understand this matter", "I am conscious of (the presence of) this piece of cloth".[20]

---

[20] *The Vedānta-Sūtras With the Commentary by Rāmānuja*, trans. George Thibaut (Delhi: Motilal Banarsidass, 1962), p. 56.

The standard Advaitin reply to this criticism, drawing upon the four-level analysis of consciousness in the *Māṇḍūkya Upaniṣad*, is that in the state of deep dreamless sleep (*suṣupti*) we do have a glimpse of this consciousness without a content. Rāmānuja rejects this analysis of the deep sleep state. When content is lost from consciousness, as when the individual passes from the waking or dreaming state into the state of deep dreamless sleep, what we say is not that he is now aware of contentless consciousness but that he is *unconscious*. As evidence Rāmānuja draws our attention to the manner in which we express the state of deep dreamless sleep to ourselves and to others. This is "by the thought presenting itself to the person risen from sleep, 'For so long a time I was not conscious of anything.'"[21] Futhermore, Rāmānuja argues that there can be no proof of a substance devoid of difference nor any meaningful talk of such a thing since all our means of valid knowledge (the *pramāṇas* of Indian philosophy) and the very language in which we express this knowledge are dependent on difference and distinction.

Thus a "pure consciousness" is indistinguishable from unconsciousness. As David Hume was later to remark about a similar conception of a divine mind:

A mind, whose acts and sentiments and ideas are not distinct and successive; one, that is wholly simple, and totally immutable; is a mind, which has no thought, no reason, no will, no sentiment, no love, no hatred; or in a word, is no mind at all. It is an abuse of terms to give it that appellation; and we may as well speak of limited extension without figure, or of number without composition.[22]

Moreover, "survival" of death conceived in terms of the continued existence of a pure contentless consciousness can apparently have no real personal relevance to an *individual*. The Advaitin eschatology seems to offer only the uninteresting promise that it is the pure contentless consciousness that persists in the state of *mokṣa*. It is these

21 Ibid., p. 53.

22 *Dialogues Concerning Natural Religion*, ed. Norman Kemp Smith, p. 159.

sorts of considerations that motivate Rāmānuja's second major line of attack upon the Advaitin position:

> To maintain that the consciousness of the "I" does not persist in the state of final release is again altogether inappropriate. It in fact amounts to the doctrine — only expressed in somewhat different words — that final release is the annihilation of the Self ... Moreover, a man who suffering pain, mental or of other kind, ... puts himself in relation to pain — "I am suffering pain" — naturally begins to reflect how he may once for all free himself from all these manifold afflictions and enjoy a state of untroubled ease; the desire of final release thus having arisen in him he at once sets to work to accomplish it. If, on the other hand, he were to realize that the effect of such activity would be the loss of personal existence, he surely would turn away as soon so somebody began to tell him about "release" ... Nor must you maintain against this that even in the state of release there persists pure consciousness; for this by no means improves your case. No sensible person exerts himself under the influence of the idea that after he himself has perished there will remain some entity termed "pure light"![23]

What can the Advaitin say in reply to these charges? Let's take Rāmānuja's second objection first. The claim is that the "survival" involved in final release (*mokṣa*) is such a bleak and empty prospect that no reasonable person would be motivated to attempt to achieve such a goal. One sort of reply to this involves an appeal to the primacy of the elimination of suffering (*duḥkha*) as an intrinsic value. Thus given that life is *duḥkha* and *mokṣa* involves freedom from *duḥkha*, *mokṣa* is worth pursuing. This is the sort of reply offered by Nyāya-Vaiśeṣika and Sāṃkhya-Yoga. In these schools it is not claimed that the liberated soul enjoys any special happiness over and above the absence of suffering. But the Advaitins reject this minimal account of *mokṣa* and assert that the liberated soul experiences a positive bliss over and above the mere cessation of suffering. Contrary to what the Naiyāyikas claim,

---

[23] *The Vedānta-Sūtras With the Commentary by Rāmānuja*, pp. 69-70.

mere cessation of suffering cannot be sufficient for the bliss of liberation promised in the scriptures. The classic Advaitin counterexample here is Maṇḍana Miśra's in the *Brahmasiddhi* (I,2). Consider the case of a man half-immersed in a cool pond in the heat of the day. The pain due to the heat over half his body has been removed but he is not happy because of the heat over his upper body that still exists. Hence bliss cannot be merely the absence of suffering.

This counterexample is uncompelling since it can easily be squared with the minimal account of *mokṣa* by insisting that "elimination of suffering" means "*complete* elimination of suffering". Nevertheless it must be conceded that the Hindu scriptures do often seem to allude to the bliss of *mokṣa* in a way that it seems forced to construe as meaning merely absence of suffering.

However the advocates of the minimal intepretation of *mokṣa* also offer a second argument for their view. If *mokṣa* is thought to be worth seeking only because it is pleasant, then it will become an object of desire. But such a desire will be counterproductive, for the desire for a permanent state of bliss is as binding as any other desire and thus a hindrance to achievement of the goal desired. The Advaitins resist this argument. Not every motivation to action involves an attachment to an object of desire. As Maṇḍana puts it (*Brahmasiddhi* I,4), not every wish (*icchā*) is passion (*rāga*), and so actions directed towards the bliss of *Brahman* are not based on passion. True, if the activity of escaping from the suffering of *saṃsāra* and reaching the bliss of *Brahman* were passion, then the achievement of *mokṣa* would be impossible. But the desire for *mokṣa* need not be so motivated. Indeed the advocate of the minimal interpretation of *mokṣa* is himself committed to the possibility of such non-attached desires, for otherwise the desire to eliminate suffering will be just as counterproductive as the desire for the bliss of *mokṣa*. In both cases the appropriate attitude towards the object of desire is one of quiet non-attachment (*vairāgya*).

In fact this debate conflates two separate questions.[24] One question is a metaphysical question: Does an individual in the state of final release really experience some sort of eternal positive pleasure? The other question is a question in ethics or

---

[24] On the importance of distinguishing these two questions and the possibility of a "Kantian" resolution of the dispute see A. Chakrabarti, "Is Liberation (*Mokṣa*) Pleasant?"

moral psychology: Should someone intent on liberation wish to attain a final state of permanent positive pleasure? Now the Advaitins respond affirmatively to both questions; the Naiyāyikas (and Sāmkhyas) respond negatively to both questions. In both cases the answer to the second question is based upon the answer to the first. However, if we insist on distinguishing these two questions, we can offer a resolution of the dispute here. That is, we can remain agnostic about the truth of the competing answers to the metaphysical question but still insist that the most reasonable answer to the psycho-ethical question is the minimal one. Given that the elimination of suffering is a basic intrinsic value, then the goal of the cessation of suffering ought to be pursued for its own sake. Whether liberation also brings with it an eternal positive happiness is a separate question that need not be answered by the aspirant to *moksa* (and very likely cannot be answered anyway). This position has a certain resemblance (which must not, however, be overemphasized) to Kant's view about the relation between virtue and happiness. The Kantian moral agent pursues virtue for its own sake; the coincidence of virtue and happiness may be a metaphysical truth, but it ought not to be a motive to moral action.

What, however, of Rāmānuja's other line of attack? Even if we concede the highly problematic existence of a pure contentless consciousness, Rāmānuja wants to insist that this consciousness would not be *me* and thus the post-mortem existence of such a disembodied consciousness could not represent *my* survival. This, of course, is the same identity problem that we have already noted as attending the notion of disembodied survival. The monistic suggestion offered by Advaita claims that there exists only one disembodied being, hence evading the problem of individuating multiple disembodied souls. However this might seem to amount to the suggestion that if I die and achieve *moksa* I will be merged with the Absolute. But then the identity claim involved in maintaining a deceased person to be now one with *Brahman* is to rest upon what criterion of identity? After all, presumably all liberated souls are one with *Brahman*. But if A and B, both deceased, are one with *Brahman*, then how can both A and B survive as distinct individuals? And if they don't survive as individuals, then what content can be given to the "survival" promised here?

The Advaitin reply here begins by insisting that the identity of the Self (*ātman*) with *Brahman* does not involve a merging of the individual with the Absolute, nor a union with God, nor the achievement of a unitive state. This *ātman/Brahman* identity already obtains, whether or not it is recognized. Properly speaking, I cannot *attain moksa*, nor *become Brahman*. *Moksa* is realizing what has always been one's innate character, but has been temporarily forgotten. The classic Advaitin illustration is the case of a king's son who, brought up as a hunter from infancy, discovers he is of royal blood.[25] This discovery involves no ontological change, for he remains what he has always been: a prince. However now he feels or realizes that he is one. Similarly, liberation is just the removal of the ignorance (*avidyā*) which hides our true nature from us.

This reply, then, involves a very bold way with the identity problem. The original problem was how to justify the claim that the liberated soul "survives" as identical with *Brahman*. In other words, what preserves identity in a process of change from life to death to *moksa*. Even if the claim that there exists only one disembodied Self is intelligible, what prevents my identity with it at *moksa* from being equivalent to the annihilation of *me* (i.e. the annihilation of my personal individuality)? The Advaitin answer is extremely radical. Firstly, *moksa* involves no ontological change in the Self and hence involves no problem about specifying what preserves identity through change. Secondly, Advaita presses home the logic of monism and denies that the individual self ceases to exist in *moksa*, for the individual self was never real in the first place! Or more precisely, the individual human person (the *jīva*) is a combination of reality and appearance. It is real insofar as *ātman* is its ground; but it is unreal insofar as it is identified as finite, conditioned, relative.

Of course, the Advaitin reply here is by no means the end of the matter. Rather it just shifts the ground of the dispute. For example, there remains a cluster of problems about the nature of the *jīva* and its relation to *ātman/Brahman*. Two influential models are offered. The first is "reflectionism" (*pratibimbavāda*), whereby the *jīva* is said to "reflect" the *ātman*. It is thus (like a reflection in a mirror) not entirely distinct from

---

[25] Cf. Śamkara's *Brhadāranyakopanisad-bhāsya*, II.1.20. The illustration is not unique to Advaita: compare *Sāmkhyasūtra*, 4.1.

the prototype, but neither is it to be identified with the prototype. The second is "limitationism" (*avacchedavāda*), whereby *ātman* is said to be like space and the individual *jīvas* like space in jars. When the jars are destroyed, the space which they enclosed remains part of space. Two important sub-schools of Advaita divide in particular upon which model to prefer: the Vivaraṇa school favours "reflectionism" and the Bhāmatī school favours "limitationism". The discussion of the merits and demerits of each model is one of the major concerns of post-Śaṃkara Advaitin dialectics.[26] However, I do not wish to pursue the intricacies of the Advaitin system any further here. Suffice it for our purposes that Advaita has resources for dealing with the identity problem as originally posed. To do so, of course, it has to construct a whole system of monistic metaphysics and epistemology, the details of which we cannot enter into here. The characteristic tenets of the system may well turn out to be false, but the developed system is too sophisticated for a charge of incoherence to be easily proven. Nevertheless it must be admitted that the possibility of disembodied immortality it offers requires a radically different conception of the nature and value of the individual self than that familiar to us from, for instance, the Judaeo-Christian tradition.

VI

We have seen, then, that the doctrine of immortality when conceived of in the form of disembodied survival of death faces a number of problems: problems, for instance, about the relation of the doctrine to dualism, and about the intelligibility of ascribing typical person-predicates to disembodied beings. These, however, do not seem insuperable. But the identity problem remains far more recalcitrant. One way to try to meet this problem is the monistic eschatology offered in Advaita Vedānta. Although apparently coherent, this scenario requires a fully developed monism and a correspondingly radical appraisal of the notion of the individual human person.

---

[26] For an interesting review of some of this argumentation see Karl H. Potter, *Presuppositions of India's Philosophies*, pp. 157-182.

There is, however, a further consideration that may make the Advaitin eschatology seem less strange than it might appear at first sight. This is to do with the *value* of immortality. Many religious traditions recognize that the religious significance of immortality cannot consist simply in endless duration; a transformed quality of post-mortem life is required. Recall also in this connection Wittgenstein's remarks about the temporal immortality of the human soul in the *Tractatus* 6.4312:

> ... but, in any case, this assumption completely fails to accomplish the purpose for which it has always been intended. Or is some riddle solved by my surviving forever? Is not this eternal life itself as much of a riddle as our present life?

But then the problem of immortality becomes twofold. On the one hand we have the *intelligibility* problem; and on the other hand, we have the *value* problem. Now in this chapter we have been basically concerned with the intelligibility question. The identity difficulty that bedevils the notion of disembodied existence is a problem about the intelligibility of one version of the doctrine of immortality. Advaita meets this difficulty at a cost, for it involves radically reconstruing the nature and value of ordinary empirical life and the individual human person.

However, it does seem that if immortality is to have any real value it must involve a transformation of ordinary mortal life. Consider, for instance, John Hick's widely discussed defence of the notion of resurrection.[27] Hick posits a doctrine of resurrection to assist with two outstanding problems: (i) to provide for the meaningfulness of religious assertions via the possibility of eschatological falsification; and (ii) to solve the problem of evil by allowing for post-mortem restitution. But in both cases the attempt to meet the attendant identity problem involves insisting on the close similarities between the ante-mortem and post-mortem lives. However, if the lives are *that* similar, then the desired resolution of the ante-mortem difficulties that the doctrine of resurrection was supposed to offer will presumably be just as unsatisfactorily

---

[27] See especially his "Theology and Verification" in Basil Mitchell, ed., *The Philosophy of Religion* (London: Oxford University Press, 1971), pp. 53-71; *Faith and Knowledge* 2nd ed., Ch. 8; *Evil and the God of Love*, Ch. 17; and *Death and Eternal Life*, particularly Chs. 8, 15.

inconclusive in the afterlife as it is in this life.[28] Price's scenario of disembodied existence, on the other hand, attempts to provide a genuinely *different* sort of afterlife; and hence faces the identity problem. There seems, then, a kind of "dilemma of immortality" here. If immortality is construed as being very like this life, we can perhaps make better sense of the identity claim involved; but the value question remains unresolved. However, if we insist on a very sharp difference between ordinary life and immortality, we can perhaps meet the value problem; but we then face the recalcitrant identity problem.

Insofar as the doctrine of immortality is supposed to have religious significance, the value problem will be felt by adherents of the doctrine to be particularly pressing. Now Advaita Vedānta is clearly a religious philosophy. Hence it is unsurprising to see it giving prominency to the value difficulty, which it tries to meet by an insistence on the essential divinity of the *ātman* and its identity with the Absolute. The eschatological picture offered, then, is one distinct from ordinary, worldly existence. This move, of course, sharpens the other horn of the dilemma in the form of the identity problem attending the notion of disembodied "survival". The Advaitin solution is radical, but apparently coherent. Its initial strangeness may be less offputting if we realize how it tries to enable its adherents to evade the "dilemma of immortality" in a consistent and religiously satisfactory way.

---

[28] To be fair to Hick it should be noted that his most recent position is that resurrection is only a possible *paraeschatology*. Ultimately the value question will have to be resolved on the level of a possible *eschatology*: compare *Death and Eternal Life*, Ch. 22.

I

In Western thought the other major traditional conception of immortality involves the notion that after death we shall be reanimated through a divine reconstitution of the bodily person. In Christianity, Judaism and Islam this is familiar as the doctrine of the resurrection of the body. Unlike the doctrine of the immortality of the soul, the doctrine of resurrection is compatible with the truth of materialism; (as also are some versions of rebirth). Hence the credibility of the doctrine is logically independent of any particular stance on the mind-body problem. Given the tenor of recent work in the philosophy of mind, this may be seen as an advantage by an advocate of the doctrine. At the very least, this feature limits the number of hostages to fortune that the doctrine has to concede. Of course, it is possible to combine a dualist account of persons with the notion of resurrection and posit an immortal soul that guarantees the identity of the dead person with the resurrectee. However, in what follows I shall be concerned with an understanding of resurrection that makes no such appeal to souls as identity guarantors. Rather resurrection will be understood as the notion of a divine reconstitution of the bodily person conceived of as a psychophysical unity. Is such a notion philosophically coherent?

Within Christianity the more traditional form of the doctrine of resurrection, dating at least from Patristic times, has been a belief in the literal resurrection of the flesh.[1] That is, after we die our bodies rot and disintegrate. But at the end of time the particles comprising each individual's flesh will be gathered together and the identical structure that death destroyed will be restored. However, this literalistic understanding of the doctrine of resurrection sits uncomfortably with what modern science tells us about the nature of matter. First, it requires the truth of an atomistic account of matter such that matter consists of eternal, incorruptible particles which persist through change. Second, the atoms which constitute me will return to the environment

---

[1] Cf. Paul Badham, *Christian Beliefs About Life After Death* (London: Macmillan, 1976), Ch. 3.

upon my death and become parts of other individuals. How can the exact atoms that constitute me at death be reassembled without berefting others? Augustine and Aquinas worried about the case of cannibals having to restore the flesh they had consumed.[2] But whereas they felt such a case to be exceptional, our current science suggests that a sharing of the "atomic" energy which is transformed into cells would seem to be the general rule. Third, a reconstitution of *exactly* the same flesh would surely be followed by a rapid second death. For whatever physical state of my body caused my original death would be duplicated by a state of my resurrected body. On this account, then, resurrection certainly will not imply immortality.

But the advocate of resurrection need not be committed to this literalistic version. Consider instead John Hick's widely discussed account of resurrection.[3] The argument proceeds via three scenarios. Firstly, suppose someone (John Smith) suddenly disappears from before the eyes of his friends at a learned gathering in London. Suppose further that simultaneously with this strange occurrence an exact "replica" of him inexplicably appears in Banaras, India. The replica "John Smith" is exactly similar to the vanished John Smith as regards bodily and mental characteristics. Moreover "John Smith" claims to remember being John Smith: at one moment listening to a paper in London, the next moment standing on Daśāśwamedha Ghāt in Banaras. Bar continuous occupancy of space, there is everything that would lead us to identify the replica "John Smith" with the vanished John Smith. Surely in such a case we would reasonably regard the "John Smith" in Banaras as the same person as the vanished John Smith.

Now consider a second scenario. This time John Smith does not disappear, but dies. Simultaneously with his death an exactly similar "John Smith" replica appears in Banaras. Notwithstanding the dead body in London, it seems reasonable to suppose that "John Smith" in Banaras is the John Smith who died, miraculously recreated in Banaras.

---

[2] See respectively *The City of God*, Bk. 22, Ch. 20 and *Summa Contra Gentiles*, 4, 80-81.

[3] See his "Theology and Verification" ; *Faith and Knowledge* 2nd ed., Ch. 8; *Death and Eternal Life*, Ch. 15; and *Philosophy of Religion* 3rd ed., pp. 124-127.

Finally, suppose that on John Smith's death the replica "John Smith" appears, not in Banaras, but as a resurrection "replica" in a resurrection world inhabited by other such resurrected "replicas". (Objects in such a world, though spatially related to each other, are in no spatial relation to objects in this world.) Once again it seems reasonable to regard the resurrected "John Smith" as the John Smith who died.

A couple of clarificatory points on all this are in order. First, the notion of plural spaces is required for the claim that the resurrection world occupies a distinct space that is in no spatial relation to this world.[4] Now there is some difficulty in the idea of temporal relations between such spatially unrelated worlds, and yet the scenario claims that the "replica" comes into existence in the resurrection world *subsequent to* the death of John Smith in this world. The special theory of relativity, however, seems to suggest that space and time are fused together into space-time in such a way that there cannot be a singular time and plural spaces. At the very least it seems that there cannot be what is a condition of the "exact replica" scenario: viz. two space-time systems subject to the same physical laws but spatially unrelated to each other. But the notion of plural spaces may not be essential to the account anyway. Hick is worried about "the absurd ... possibility of, for example, radio communication or rocket travel between earth and heaven."[5] Positing divine recreation in another galaxy will meet this difficulty, though there then remain certain practical problems about the number of planets available that possess suitable biospheres.[6]

Secondly, the term "replica" (placed by Hick in quotes) is a term of art:

> The quotes are intended to mark a difference between the normal concept of a replica and the more specialized concept in use here. The paradigm sense of "replica" is that in which there is an original object ... of which a more or less exact copy is then made. It is logically possible ... for the original and the replica to exist simultaneously; and also for there to be any number of replicas of the same original. In contrast to this ... it is not logically possible

---

[4] On the possibility of plural spaces see Anthony Quinton, "Spaces and Times" *Philosophy* 37 (1962): 130-147.

[5] *Faith and Knowledge*, p. 185.

[6] Cf. Badham, pp. 70-71, 78-79.

for the original and the "replica" to exist simultaneously or for there to be more than one "replica" of the same original. If a putative "replica" did exist simultaneously with its original it would not be a "replica" but a replica; and if there were more than one they would not be "replicas" but replicas.[7]

As we shall see, this point will be important in relation to a particular objection to Hick's view.

II

What, then, are we to say about this version of resurrection? Well, the obvious question is: Will the "replica" resurrectee really be *me*? And indeed this is an old worry about the idea of resurrection: it concerned Aquinas, for instance, in the *Summa Contra Gentiles* (4, 80-81). How can we distinguish my survival of death through resurrection from my extinction followed by the creation of a being that is not me though it resembles me to the highest degree? There are two lines of objection to the account of resurrection offered above, both of which are generated by a concern with this question. Firstly, it is objected that the "replica" will not be me, or at least it will not unambiguously be me. Secondly, it is claimed that unless the "replica" is unambiguously me, the "survival" of such a being after my death cannot reasonably be of any real interest to me. Let's examine these objections more closely.

In the first place consider the following argument designed to show that the "replica" could not be the same person as the deceased.[8] If it is possible that God might create a resurrected "John Smith", then it is also possible that He might create two or

---

[7] *Death and Eternal Life*, p. 283.

[8] This objection derives from an argument employed in a somewhat different context by Bernard Williams: see his *Problems of the Self*, Ch. 1. For applications of this argument to Hick's theory see J. J. Clarke, "John Hick's Resurrection" *Sophia* **10** (3) (1971): 18-22; and J. J. Lipner, "Hick's Resurrection" *Sophia* **18** (3) (1979): 22-34. This "duplicate objection" is prefigured in the writings of the eighteenth century freethinker Antony Collins. Collins utilizes a Lockean account of personal identity and then raises the duplicate objection to cause problems for the traditional doctrine of the resurrection: see Samuel Clarke, *The Works 1738*, Vol. 3, (New York: Garland, 1978), pp. 877-879.

more "John Smiths"; (call them "JS_2", "JS_3" etc.). However, JS_2 and JS_3 cannot both be identical with the original John Smith (JS_1), otherwise (by the transitivity and symmetry of identity) JS_2 and JS_3 would be identical with each other. Thus if we had a JS_3, then this would prevent us identifying JS_2 (or JS_3) as the same person as JS_1. Furthermore, the mere *possibility* of such a duplicate precludes identifying JS_2 with JS_1, even if we have no JS_3. Otherwise we could have a situation where JS_2 is identical with JS_1 today but tomorrow (when God creates JS_3) JS_2, though identical with the JS_2 of today, will cease to be identical with JS_1. Again, suppose God creates JS_2 while JS_1 is still alive. Why will JS_2 "become" JS_1 when JS_1 dies, but not before?

It is to block this sort of objection that Hick insists on his special use of the term "replica". "Replica", it will be recalled, is defined so that there cannot be more than one "replica" of a given individual at any one time. Of course, Hick does not want to make his victory over his opponent here a merely verbal one. Hence he concedes that if there were two resurrection JS's, then neither of them could be identical with the deceased JS_1. However he denies that the unrealized logical possibility of such duplication makes it impossible for there to be one resurrection "replica" that could be identified with the dead JS_1. In other words, Hick incorporates a uniqueness condition into his account such that a perfect replica is only a "replica" if it is unique. And only a "replica" can be the same person as the deceased.

But this reply will not satisfy the opponent. His objection, he insists, is still unanswered. Suppose, for instance, that after JS_1 dies God creates a "replica" JS_2 who is thus identifiable as the same person as JS_1. Some time later, however God creates JS_3. At this point JS_2 presumably ceases to be the same person as JS_1. Again, suppose that after some further time JS_3 goes out of existence. Does JS_2 now again become the same person as JS_1? These conclusions are surely unacceptable.

The point of these examples, of course, is to reinforce a general argumentative strategy which tries to show that there cannot be a particular unique entity by showing that there could be two or more such entities. Underlying this is an implicit appeal to a principle (call it the "independence principle") such that an entity's identity cannot depend upon the existence of any other entity. This principle in turn implies another principle (call it the "uniqueness principle") to the effect that if there could be another entity such that identity did not obtain at some particular time, then identity never obtains, even if this possible other entity is never actualized.

Both principles, however, are unsatisfactory. Suppose Y at t_2 is identifiable with X at t_1, in virtue of the fulfilment of some condition C. Now it will be true that if two candidates for identity with X both fulfil C, then neither can be X in virtue of fulfilling C. However this doesn't imply that the fulfilment of C isn't good grounds for identifying Y at t_2 with X at t_1 in the first case. For example: a particular present amoeba is identifiable with a past amoeba on the grounds of spatio-temporal continuity. However, suppose the amoeba undergoes mitosis and splits into two identical twins. Let's concede *per argumentum* that in such a case to identify either of the twins with the previous amoeba would be unjustifiable, even though both twins are spatio-temporally continuous with the previous amoeba. But this concession does not in turn do anything to undermine the adequacy of spatio-temporal continuity as (sufficient) grounds for the identity judgement in the non-mitosis case.[9] What is important in such cases about judgements of identity is not the uniformity of features possessed by all the candidates involved, but rather the exclusion of the multiplication of contenders for identity. In other words, the identity judgement invokes a uniqueness condition that excludes there being any competitors, just as Hick insists with his special use of "replica". And since there is nothing so odd about this in other (non-resurrection) cases of identification, the independence principle and its cognate the uniqueness principle are rendered implausible. Thus the argument from the putative possibility of duplication to the impossibility of resurrection fails.

III

We have seen, then, that the objection that the resurrection "replica" could not be reasonably identified with the deceased person is unjustified. However, there still remains a more moderate claim: viz. that the resurrectee is not unambiguously the same person as the deceased. That is, while it is open to us to identify the resurrectee

---

[9] Cf. R. T. Herbert, *Paradox and Identity in Theology* (Ithaca: Cornell University Press, 1979), pp. 144-146.

with the deceased, this option is merely permissible, not mandatory. We certainly can decide to regard the resurrectee as the same person as the deceased. Moreover, there seems no compelling reason for saying that the resurrectee is not identifiable with the ante-mortem person in this way. However, neither is there any compelling reason for saying that they have to be so identified. Thus the description of something as important as the future life is left in a state of irreducible ambiguity.[10]

Hick himself is untroubled by this objection since he believes that "*all* cases other than straightforward everyday identity require a decision."[11] Thus that the resurrection-world cases demand linguistic legislation is no special problem. His contention is that the decision to identify the resurrectee with the ante-mortem person would be more reasonable and less problematic than a decision to regard them as different people. A defence of the reasonableness of such a decision would presumably then involve a holistic approach attempting to balance the advantages and disadvantages of such a decision given other beliefs, frequency of such cases etc.

Now some will undoubtedly have qualms about the conventionalist tenor of Hick's approach here. At the very least it would be happier if the post-mortem situation could be made unambiguous, (as even Hick would surely admit). One attempt to do just this has been offered by Robert Herbert.[12] His argument is that the purported ambiguity can be resolved by reference to God's intentions. He proposes an analogy with the case of a Wyeth painting about which you are undecided as to whether it is a portrait of Robert Frost or of George C. Marshall. The ambiguity is resolved when you learn from Wyeth that he intended to paint Frost. Similarly, God's intention to resurrect the dead makes the act God performs into an act of recreating the dead. Of course, in the absence of knowledge of God's intention it would be reasonable to interpret the resurrection situation differently. However, knowledge of God's intentions (presumably gained through revelation) makes the situation unambiguous.

---

[10] This is Terence Penelhum's position: see his *Survival and Disembodied Existence*, Ch. 9; and "Survival and Identity: Some Recent Discussions", pp. 47-49.

[11] *Death and Eternal Life*, p. 288.

[12] Herbert, pp. 149-155.

This attempt, however, is unconvincing. In the first place it cannot be that a painter's intention to produce a portrait of Frost can make the painting he produces a portrait *of Frost*. Intentions can misfire. Suppose I intend to paint a portrait of Frost and then produce something otherwise indistinguishable from traditional depictions of Santa Claus. Does my intention that my painting be a portrait of Frost make it a portrait of Frost? Surely what has happened is that I intended to paint a portrait of Frost and failed. Moreover what I have produced is better described as a painting of Santa Claus. Thus my intention that my painting be a portrait of Frost is neither sufficient nor necessary for my producing a portrait of Frost.

Of course, it may be replied that the analogy is importantly different in the case of resurrection. God's omnipotence presumably precludes the possibility of any failed divine intentions. However, the argument also faces a second difficulty. The claim is that what makes the portrait unambiguously a portrait of Frost is the painter's intention that the portrait be (unambiguously) a portrait of Frost. Similarly God's intention to recreate the dead person makes the resurrectee unambiguously the same person as the deceased. But this is obviously circular. Our original problem was to give an account of what would count as an unambiguous case of resurrection of the dead. An answer of the form "A case where God intended the resurrectee to be unambiguously a resurrection of the deceased person" is useless unless we already independently understand what it would be like for a resurrectee to be unambiguously identifiable with a dead person. But this is precisely the notion in need of explication.

A rather different approach to this task of making unambiguous the situation is to challenge the assumption that the resurrection situation is ambiguous in the first place.[13] To describe the resurrection situation as ambiguous is to beg the question against the doctrine of resurrection by assuming that the notion of a person is not gap-inclusive, i.e. that we cannot have a person whose history includes a stretch of nothingness. Now we certainly have other gap-inclusive entities (plays, wars etc.) that extend over time. Why can't the concept of a person be the concept of a gap-inclusive entity in this way? Indeed the theist who supports the doctrine of resurrection (and this includes, of course, many Christians, Jews and Muslims) is already working with a

---

[13] Ibid., pp. 155-160.

concept of a person as a gap-inclusive being. Hence the resurrection scenario is not ambiguous so far as he or she is concerned.

However this approach just leaves us with another standoff. On this account the believer and the sceptic have different concepts of what a person is and in accordance with these concepts neither finds the resurrection situation genuinely ambiguous, though each differs in his or her interpretation of the situation. How, then, are we to arbitrate this dispute about the proper understanding of the concept of a person? Presumably once again the arguments for the competing concepts of a person will have to be holistically weighted in terms of their plausibility relative to other beliefs, frequency of puzzle cases etc. In other words, we are left with much the same ambiguity as Hick originally admitted and much the same inconclusiveness with regard to how to weight the factors that could settle the matter one way or the other.

IV

So far, then, I have argued that there is no reason why the resurrectee could not be the same person as the deceased. However, given the resurrection scenario we have been considering, it does seem true that the resurrectee is not unambiguously the same person as the deceased. Well, so what? Why does this matter?

One answer to this question is offered, in a characteristically forthright fashion, by Antony Flew:

> For thus to produce even the most indistinguishably similar object after the first one has been totally destroyed and disappeared is to produce not the same object again, but a replica. To punish or to reward a replica, reconstituted on Judgement Day, for the sins or the virtues of the old Antony Flew dead and cremated in 1984 is as inept and as unfair as it would be to reward or punish one identical twin for what was in fact done by the other.[14]

---

14 Antony Flew, *The Presumption of Atheism*, p. 107.

This objection, however, is uncompelling. Firstly, to try to utilize it against Hick's theory would be to beg the question by assuming that Hick's "replica" is really only a replica. On Hick's account "replica" resurrectees (unlike identical twins) *are* the same persons as those they are exact replicas of. Secondly, even if the "replica" was not identical with the deceased, the immorality of punishing or rewarding such a replica is dependent upon the truth of a retributivist account of punishment. Of course, it might be true that any adequate theory of just punishment must be at least partially retributivist. All I want to point out at the moment is that the charge of immorality is only as strong as the thesis of retributivism. On competing deterrence or reformative theories of punishment the punishment of replicas may be justifiable in certain circumstances. Moreover, if the argument is used as as *ad hominem* one against Hick, then it surely misfires. Traditional Christianity is strongly retributivist, but Hick's espousal of universal salvation and his "soul making" theodicy square better with a non-retributivist account of punishment.

But it is surely a deeper belief about the importance of unambiguous identity that is at issue here. Roughly speaking it amounts to this: Unless the resurrectee is unambiguously *me*, then *I* won't survive death; and unless it is unambiguously *me* that survives, then the resurrection situation is not one *I* should reasonably be concerned about. Put baldly in this way the objection clearly rests upon some version of what I shall call the "egoistic principle". Notwithstanding its popularity, the egoistic principle is difficult to formulate precisely. Moreover, it admits of strong and weak versions. A strong version would be a claim to the effect that it is only reasonable to act in our own self-interests and to be concerned just with what happens to ourselves in the future. A weak version would be that it is somehow especially rational to act in our own self-interests and to be primarily concerned with just what happens to us in the future.

Some philosophers have felt that egoism, far from being a rational view, is in fact irrational in the strong sense of being self-contradictory. This was, for instance, G.E. Moore's view in *Principia Ethica* (sects. 59-60). However it is doubtful that egoism can really be shown to be irrational in this strong sense.[15] Nevertheless it does seem appropriate to challenge the assumption that even the weak version of the egoistic principle is self-evidently rational. Why is it any more reasonable for me to be especially concerned about my future happiness than about the happiness of others? Indeed on egoistic principles it is unclear that it is even rational to concern myself with the happiness of my future selves. This point was well made by Sidgwick:

> I do not see why the axiom of Prudence should not be questioned, when it conflicts with present inclination, on a ground similar to that on which Egoists refuse to admit the axiom of Rational Benevolence. If the Utilitarian has to answer the question, "Why should I sacrifice my own happiness for the greater happiness of another?" it must surely be admissible to ask the Egoist, "Why should I sacrifice a present pleasure for a greater one in the future? Why should I concern myself about my own future feelings any more than about the feelings of other persons?"[16]

In other words, let's assume what is in fact the dominant empiricist account of the self: viz. that the self is not a uniform substance that persists through time, but rather a cluster of past, present and future "selves" connected to each other by ties of various degrees.[17] Now what reason does my present (egoistic) self have for promoting the interests of any of my future selves? Of course, it is true that if we analyse a person as a series of causally related selves stretching over time, then my future selves will be causally related to my present self in a way that the future selves of others will not be related to my present self. However, in the first place some of my distant future selves will be much less closely tied to my present self than my immediately succeeding future selves will be. So why consider the interests of my distant future selves as

---

[15] Cf. C. D. Broad, "Certain Features in Moore's Ethical Doctrines" in Paul Arthur Schilpp, ed., *The Philosophy of G. E Moore* (Evanston: Northwestern University, 1942), pp. 43-57; and Bob Durrant, "Is Egoism A Possible Morality?" in R. G. Durrant, ed., *Essays in Honour of Gwen Taylor* (Dunedin: Philosophy Department, University of Otago, 1982), pp. 36-51.

[16] Henry Sidgwick, *The Methods of Ethics* 7th ed. (New York: Dover, 1966), p. 418.

[17] This view of the self, though currently popular, has not gone unchallenged: see, for example, Geoffrey Madell, *The Identity of the Self* (Edinburgh: Edinburgh University Press, 1981).

meriting consideration over the interests of my immediately succeeding future selves, as indeed I so often prudentially do? Secondly, why should this causal link matter anyway? Why does the fact that my future selves are part of a causal series of selves of which my present self is a member provide any reason for my present self to be concerned with other members of this series, any more than the members of any other series?

Hence it seems that a certain minimal altruism is required for prudential egoistic action; the promotion of the interests of my future selves is a minimally altruistic act (especially when such interests clash with my present desires). And this is surely not so surprising an idea as all that. After all, the common sense attitude (at least in our culture) is neither purely egoistic nor purely altruistic. Rather it is what Broad has called "self-referential altruism".[18] That is, it admits the rationality (and even the obligatoriness) of a concern for the interests of others, but for others that have some special connection with oneself (relatives, friends, colleagues etc.). As Broad puts it:

> Each person may be regarded as a centre of a number of concentric circles.
> The persons and the groups to whom he has the most urgent obligations may
> be regarded as forming the innermost circle. Then comes a circle of persons
> and groups to whom his obligations are moderately urgent. Finally there is
> the outermost circle of persons (and animals) to whom he has only the
> obligation of "common humanity".[19]

On this common sense view, then, the rationality of concern for (and obligation to) other selves is a function of their "distance" from oneself (or one's present self). A self's distance from my present self is in turn, I suggest, a function of its overall similarity to my present self. An analogy with possible world metaphysics is useful here.[20] Suppose we conceive of other possible worlds as radiating in various directions from the actual world at a particular time. Now those worlds closest to the

---

[18] Broad, p. 51.

[19] Ibid., p. 55.

[20] Cf. Eddy M. Zemach, "Love Thy Neighbour as Thyself or Egoism and Altruism" in Peter A. French *et al.*, eds., *Studies in Ethical Theory* (Morris: University of Minnesota, 1978), p. 157.

actual world constitute its immediate neighbours, distance from the actual world being a function of overall similarity to it. To measure X's distance from Y in the actual world W is to measure how far X has to go in possibility space before it is indistinguishable from Y in W.

Now on this model it is clear that the unambiguous identity of the resurrectee with the deceased is largely irrelevant to the question of the rationality of a concern with the fate of the resurrectee. An exactly similar resurrectee may be "closer" to my present self than certain of my descendant or ancestral selves. On the common sense view of self-referential altruism, then, it is entirely rational to concern myself with the fate of an exactly similar resurrectee, whether or not the resurrectee is unambiguously identical with me.

V

The thrust of the previous argument, of course, is an attempt to undercut the assumption of the *importance* of self-identity. In other words, to suggest that the strong sense of metaphysical identity is not the relation that really ought to matter to us. It happens that in our world identity seems a necessary condition of the connectedness that really concerns us, i.e. the psychological connectedness which is (at least partially) a function of similarity. But this is a contingent matter; we should not mistake our concern with the latter relation for a concern with the former. The point at issue here can be highlighted by consideration of one of the standard "puzzle cases" about personal identity: viz. the possibility of fission.

Let's suppose that we have an individual A existing at a time t_1. At a later time t_2, however, A fissions into B and C. B and C are exactly similar to each other and to A. Now how is A related to B and C? There are various possible replies. Firstly, we might want to say that A is B (or C), but not both B and C.[21] And yet B and C are exactly similar, so on what grounds could we distinguish between either's claim to be A? Secondly, we might want to say that both B and C are A, but B and C are not to be

---

[21] Cf. Roderick M. Chisholm, *Person and Object* (London: George Allen & Unwin, 1976), pp. 111-112.

identified with each other.[22] This, of course, involves a heroic denial of either the symmetry or the transitivity of identity. Thirdly, we might want to say that neither *B* nor *C* is *A*, notwithstanding exact similarity and spatio-temporal continuity.[23]

Each of these proposed answers involves a common assumption: viz. that there must be a correct answer to the identity question in such a case. Moreover the concern with attempting to answer the identity question involves a second assumption: viz. that the identity relation is the important relation in such a case. Both assumptions have been challenged by Derek Parfit.[24] Not only is it implausible to insist that there *must* be a correct answer to the identity question in the fission case, but insofar as we are concerned with the identity question in order to decide whether *A* survives or fails to survive the fission, then our concern is misplaced. The survival question is independent of the identity question; what matters for survival need not be identity. Rather what is important is the relation of psychological connectedness, which is not a one-one relation like identity, but a similarity relation that admits of degrees. Thus in the fission case *A* survives as both *B* and *C*, even though *B* and *C* are not identical with each other nor with *A*.

The relevance of this for the doctrine of resurrection is obvious.[25] That the resurrectee is not unambiguously identical with the deceased is irrelevant for survival. If the resurrectee is an exact replica of the deceased then we have psychological continuity with a special cause (God's willing to create the resurrectee). Such resurrection is as good as (or as bad as) survival. Nor need the spectre of duplicate resurrectees faze us. Hick's account of resurrection, of course, incorporates a uniqueness condition such that a genuine resurrectee must be unique. But this condition is only necessary if we wish our account of resurrection to preserve strict identity, as Hick does. If, however, we distinguish the notions of identity and survival,

---

[22] Cf. Arthur N. Prior, *Papers in Logic and Ethics* (London: Duckworth, 1976), Ch. 6; and *Papers on Time and Tense* (Oxford: Clarendon Press, 1968), Ch. 8.

[23] Cf. Bernard Williams, *Problems of the Self*, Chs. 1-2. Williams actually denies that in the case of fission spatio-temporal continuity is preserved (p. 24).

[24] See his "Personal Identity"; "On 'The Importance of Self-Identity'"; "Later Selves and Moral Principles"; and *Reasons and Persons*, Part Three.

[25] Cf. "On 'The Importance of Self-Identity'", pp. 689-690.

then multiple exactly similar resurrectees can all be seen as survivors of the deceased, even if such resurrectees are not (and cannot be) identical with the deceased.

One way of clarifying what is being claimed here is suggested by a consideration of Benjamin Franklin's epitaph, composed by Franklin himself and now inscribed near his grave in Philadelphia:

> The body of B. Franklin, Printer, Like the Cover of an old Book, Its Contents torn out, And stript of its Lettering and Gilding, Lies here, Food for Worms. But the work shall not be lost; for it will, as he believ'd, appear once more in a new and more elegant Edition Corrected and improved By the Author.[26]

Commenting on this sentiment, Flew objects:

> ... the Creator might very well choose to issue a Second edition — "Corrected and improved by the Author" — of Benjamin Franklin. But the Second Edition, however welcome, would by the same token not be the original Signer.[27]

Now this would surely be a curious objection if we were really talking about literary works. My copy of *David Copperfield* is, in a perfectly familiar sense, the same novel as your copy of *David Copperfield*. Moreover, different editions of the work are also nonetheless the same novel. A popular way of explicating this feature of literary works is to invoke Peirce's type/token distinction. Thus the novel *David Copperfield* is a type of which particular copies of the novel are tokens. For most of our literary purposes all we require is the preservation of type-identity; it is not generally essential to preserve token-identity (though for certain antiquarian purposes this may be considered relevant).

---

[26] Quoted in Flew, *The Presumption of Atheism*, p. 107.
[27] Ibid.

What I propose is that we should take over the hint implicit in Franklin's epitaph and apply the type/token distinction to the concept of a person.[28] On this account, then, what I am is a token of a person-type. Thus one way to construe the resurrection scenario would be to understand my resurrectee to be a distinct token of the same type. (This is not, of course, the only way to construe the scenario. Given a gap-inclusive conception of a person, the resurrectee may be a part of the same token of the person-type.) However, if we do introduce the type/token distinction here then the question, "Will I be the same person as the resurrectee?" is systematically ambiguous between type-identity and token-identity. This systematic ambiguity is concealed from us by the contingent fact that in our world each person-type happens to have associated with it at any particular time only one correlative token. But this is not a necessary truth; God could organize things differently, in which case we could have multiple resurrectees. Such resurrectees would be type-identical with the deceased, but not token-identical.

One advantage of this view is that type-identity can be preserved even though individual tokens are not exactly similar in all respects. Three Volkswagens, for example, can all be tokens of the same Volkswagen-type without each of these three tokens having to be exactly similar to each other in every other respect. This feature of type/token identity conditions allows for certain eschatological views that have traditionally been associated with the resurrection doctrine in Western religious thought. It allows, in other words, room for the resurrection token to be an improvement upon the deceased token, even though a token of the same type. On this account, then, survival can include the religious possibility that the resurrection life allows for an opportunity for growth, purification and spiritual advance. Moreover, this point about type/token identity meets the objection that the identical resurrectee would have to perish immediately; type-identity does not require absolutely exact similarity. Similarly for the traditional worry about what age the resurrectee would be.[29]

---

[28] The relevance of the type/token distinction for a Parfitian account of survival is also maintained in Andrew Brennan, "Personal Identity and Personal Survival" *Analysis* **42** (1982): 44-50; and "Survival" *Synthese* **59** (1984): 339-361. (Compare too Williams, pp. 80-81).

[29] A traditional medieval answer was thirty-two years and three months, i.e. the same age as Christ at his death: see John Hick, *Death and Eternal Life*, p. 296.

One obvious objection to the theory proposed is that type-identity isn't close enough to matter. This involves once again an implicit appeal to the egoistic principle. But we have already cast doubt upon that principle in favour of self-referential altruism. And surely on the latter theory type-identity is sufficiently close a similarity relation for it to be reasonable to concern oneself with other tokens of the same person-type as oneself. However, for the stronger claim that preservation of type-identity is as good as survival, even if token-identity is not necessarily maintained, we need to introduce a further causal condition. For A to survive as B, B must not merely be type-identical with A, but must also be causally related to A in such a way that this causal link explains B's possession of properties previously possessed by A. A mundane example of the sort of causal explanation envisaged here may help. Suppose I crash my car, damaging it badly. It goes into a garage for repairs and some time later it is returned to me in as new condition. Or is it? In fact the repairs on the car have been so extensive that the scrupulous metaphysician now has doubts that the repaired car is the same token as the car involved in the accident. Nevertheless it is clear that type-identity has been preserved. And surely this, together with the appropriate causal link, is sufficient for the claim that the repaired car is for all practical intents and purposes the same car (or at least as good as the same car). Indeed motorists seem typically to presuppose the reasonableness of this claim when they insure their cars. The damaged car, then, survives as the repaired car. The resurrection case is analogous, only there the appropriate causal explanation will, of course, be in terms of God's agency.

The other obvious worry about the theory is the degree of ontological commitment it involves. Now it is possible to construe the type/token distinction platonistically so that it is just another version of the universal/particular distinction. On this construal the utilization of the type/token distinction might seem to commit us at least to the existence of universals, though not necessarily to a full-blooded realism about such universals. Some philosophers would then consider the ontological price of the theory too high to be attractive. However, such nominalistic scruples are misplaced because the type/token distinction has to be accepted by *everyone*, whatever account may be given of it. Thus there is a dilemma here. If there is an adequate nominalist account of the type/token distinction then there can be no nominalistic objection to the resurrection theory utilizing this distinction. On the other hand, if no adequate nominalist account of the type/token distinction can be given, then this is an objection to nominalism and not to the resurrection theory that utilizes the distinction.

VI

I have argued, then, for the coherence of the doctrine of resurrection, understood as the notion of a divine reconstitution of the bodily person without appeal to any immortal soul as an identity guarantor. Such a view of resurrection has been urged, for example, by John Hick and in the first part of this chapter I have defended his sort of account against certain misconceived objections. However, in the latter half of this chapter I have proposed what is in some ways a more radical theory which attempts to undercut the assumption of the importance of strict metaphysical identity and to explicate the notion of survival in terms of the type/token distinction. Of course, it should be understood that here I have only been concerned to defend the *metaphysical* coherence of the doctrine of resurrection. Thus there still remain other philosophical questions about the doctrine: *epistemic* questions, for instance, about whether we have ever had (or could have) evidence to believe that resurrection has actually taken place, and *value* questions about the meaningfulness of God's resurrecting us for an eternal life. (Broadly speaking these questions are special cases of traditional philosophical problems about the epistemology of miracles and the meaning and value of life.) However, these other questions, notwithstanding that they are related to the metaphysical question, are nonetheless distinct. Discussion of them falls outside of my present brief in this chapter (though I have already tried to say something about the second of these two questions in Chapters 4 and 5).

CHAPTER 8: REBIRTH

I

Traditional Western conceptions of immortality characteristically presume that we come into existence at a particular time (birth or conception), live out our earthly span and then die. According to some, our death may then be followed by a deathless post-mortem existence. In other words, it is assumed that (i) we are born only once and die only once; and (ii) that (at least on some accounts) we are future-sempiternal creatures. The Western secular tradition affirms at least (i); the Western religious tradition (Christianity, Judaism, Islam) generally affirms both (i) and (ii). The Indian tradition, however, typically denies both (i) and (ii). That is, it maintains both that we all have pre-existed beginninglessly, and that we have lived many times before and must live many times again in this world. The Indian picture, then, is that we have died and been reborn innumerable times previous to this life and (failing our undertaking some spiritual discipline) we will be reborn many times in the future. This is sometimes called the Indian belief in reincarnation. The difficulty with this usage is that the term "reincarnation" suggests a belief in an immortal soul that transmigrates or reincarnates. However Buddhism, while affirming rebirth, specifically denies the existence of an eternal soul. Thus the term "rebirth" is preferable for referring to the generally espoused Indian doctrine.

Of course, the fact that the doctrine of rebirth is fundamental to Indian religious thought (including Hinduism, Buddhism, Jainism and Sikhism) is widely known in the West.[1] However it is symptomatic of the ethnocentrism of contemporary analytic

---

[1] An excellent locus for material on Indian views is Wendy Doniger O'Flaherty, ed., *Karma and Rebirth in Classical Indian Traditions* (Berkeley: University of California Press, 1980). The idea of rebirth is, of course, by no means confined to India: compare the selections in Joseph Head and S. L. Cranston, eds., *Reincarnation in World Thought* (New York: Julian Press, 1967). For a recent attempt to rehabilitate reincarnation within Christianity see Geddes MacGregor, *Reincarnation as a Christian Hope* (London: Macmillan, 1982).

philosophy of religion that the vast majority of philosophers in this tradition continue
to ignore Indian religious concepts and prefer to concentrate almost exclusively on
Judaeo-Christian religious notions.[2] A typical example of this parochial trend is
provided by Peter Geach who prefaces what is, in certain respects, a quite interesting
essay on reincarnation with the following demurral:

> ... I shall not try to discuss any Hindu or Buddhist views. This may strike
> some people as frivolous, in the way that it would be frivolous for
> somebody writing philosophical theology to discuss the writings of Judge
> Rutherford rather than of Thomas Aquinas. No doubt Hindu and Buddhist
> writings about reincarnation are of more inherent interest than *The Search
> for Bridey Murphy*; but I am wholly incompetent to discuss them; and even
> if I were myself able to talk about *atman* or *karma*, these are not notions
> which many of my readers could readily deploy.[3]

The argument is instructive: Geach himself is innocent of Indian views of
rebirth; so too are most of his readers; therefore it is better for everyone to remain in
this blessed state of innocence. Of course, an unkind critic might suggest that this
cognitive innocence is just plain ignorance. Couple this suggestion with the common
Indian belief that it is ignorance (*avidyā*) which is the cause of bondage to suffering
and we have the beginnings of a case for treating Indian views about rebirth less
cavalierly. Anyway, in this chapter I propose to take the Indian doctrine of rebirth to
be a serious metaphysical hypothesis and to consider critically the question of the
philosophical credibility of such a doctrine.

---

[2] One notable exception is to be found in the recent writings of John Hick: see especially his *Death
and Eternal Life*, Chs. 16-19; and *Philosophy of Religion* 3rd ed., Ch. 10. However the foremost
pioneer in this regard is probably Ninian Smart, who has often discussed Indian views in various of
his many publications, beginning with *Reasons and Faiths* (London: Routledge & Kegan Paul,
1958).

[3] Peter Geach, *God and the Soul*, p. 2.

II

Briefly there are two sorts of arguments that can be offered for the rebirth theory: viz. philosophical arguments and empirical arguments. The first category includes metaphysical, ethical and theological arguments for the thesis; the second category presents the thesis as an explanatory hypothesis that satisfactorily accounts for various empirical phenomena. In practice the two types of argument can be rather difficult to separate. However, it is clear that for the thesis to serve as an adequate explanatory hypothesis it must at least be metaphysically coherent. Hence it is appropriate to begin by considering some metaphysical arguments for the truth of the rebirth thesis.

As I have already indicated, the Indian doctrine of rebirth includes both a belief in post-existence (I will be born again after my death) and a belief in pre-existence (my present life was preceded by a previous existence and so on). These two beliefs are in fact logically distinct. Nevertheless they are mutually supportive. Hence if I pre-existed in a previous life, then I have survived death once and it is not unreasonable to suppose I might survive death again. Similarly, if I am presently post-existing relative to a previous life, then my previous life might also have involved post-existence relative to a yet earlier life — and so on. Finally, if I will post-exist in a succeeding life, then it is not unreasonable to suppose that I will die in that life and be reborn again. Thus pre-existence and post-existence together make probable (but do not entail) the Indian doctrine of a beginningless plurality of lives. Moreover, any metaphysical evidence for the truth of post-existence would seem also to favour the truth of pre-existence, and vice versa.[4] (Once again, however, it must be admitted that there seems no straightforward entailment relation involved here.)

In any case, the doctrine of pre-existence is certainly part of the Indian view of rebirth and so it is important to examine arguments for the truth of the doctrine. Now most Indian philosophers have believed (as most Indians still do) that we all have pre-

---

[4] Similar conclusions are urged in J. M. E. McTaggart, *Some Dogmas of Religion*, Ch. 4; and *The Nature of Existence*, Vol. 2 (Cambridge: Cambridge University Press, 1927), Ch. 63. However, much of McTaggart's argumentation concerning pre-existence and post-existence is inextricably connected with the special peculiarities of his own metaphysical system.

existed beginninglessly. Indeed, since only the defunct Cārvāka school maintained otherwise, classical Indian philosophy displays a relative paucity of arguments for this thesis when compared with the extensive body of discussion it offers about the nature of what it is that has pre-existed.[5] Thus there are some empirical arguments adduced, like the Naiyāyika appeal to the inborn inclination of infants to suckle and their fears and joys.[6] These, however, may be uncompelling in the light of modern biological theory. There are also certain theological arguments related to the efficacy of the thesis in explaining away the problem of evil.[7] But these require for their plausibility prior commitment to a theistic point of view. More interesting philosophically are certain metaphysical arguments that purport to establish the pre-existence thesis. I want to examine critically two such attempts: one by the eighth century Indian Buddhist philosopher Śāntaraksita and one by an outstanding modern Western interpreter of Indian philosophy, Karl H. Potter.

Śāntaraksita's argument (glossed by his pupil Kamalaśīla) appears in his remarkable polemical compendium, the *Tattvasangraha* (*ślokas* 1857-1964).[8] The chapter in question is devoted to a refutation of the views of the materialist Lokāyatas. It is important to understand, however, that this argument for pre-existence is not an argument for the pre-existence of a soul, i.e. an enduring substantial entity underlying change. Indeed, as a Buddhist Śāntaraksita is committed to the denial of any such entity. Rather he assumes a particular Buddhist account of a person as a series of causally efficient point-instants. According to some Buddhist philosophers this person-series includes both mental and physical events or states. Hence for them a

---

[5] For a review of some of these arguments see Ninian Smart, *Doctrine and Argument in Indian Philosophy* (London: George Allen & Unwin, 1964), Ch. 12.

[6] *Nyāyasūtra* III.1.18, 21. There is a brief discussion of these arguments in Karl H. Potter, ed., *Indian Metaphysics and Epistemology: The Tradition of Nyāya-Vaiśesika up to Gangeśa* (Princeton: Princeton University Press, 1977), pp. 35-37.

[7] On these sorts of arguments see Arthur L. Herman, *The Problem of Evil and Indian Thought* (Delhi: Motilal Banarsidass, 1976), Part III.

[8] See *The Tattvasangraha of Śāntaraksita with the Commentary of Kamalaśīla*, Vol. 2, trans. Ganganatha Jha (Baroda: Oriental Institute, 1939), pp. 887-935. This seems to be the unspecified source for the "Buddhist Idealist" argument cited in Smart, *Doctrine and Argument in Indian Philosophy*, pp. 160-161.

person is a two-strand causal series comprising both a chain of physical events and a chain of mental events. The two chains are related co-ordinately (*sādṛśya*) but not causally: a view similar to the theory of psycho-physical parallelism in Western philosophy.[9] However Śāntarakṣita seems to favour an idealist account at various points, in which case the person is presumably to be identified with the chain of mental events. Either way, the argument is an argument for the pre-existence of the consciousness series.

The argument rests upon two principles. The first is the principle of universal causation, i.e. that every event has a cause. The second is a principle to the effect that not every mental event is totally caused by physical events. Or more exactly, that there are some mental events which have no physical events in their causal ancestry (allowing here for the possibility of indirect causation). Call this the "mental cause principle". (Note that this formulation of the mental cause principle is compatible with either a realist or an idealist ontology.) These two principles can then be used to generate the following argument. For consider the first member of the chain of cognitions. Or more precisely, consider the first mental state in the life of an individual that is not totally caused by physical states. It must have as at least its part-cause a mental state occurring before the birth (or conception) of the individual. Thus pre-existence is established. Moreover, since this argument can be repeated for any previous life, the beginninglessness of the causal series of cognitions is established. Finally, since there is a previous birth, it is also reasonable to assume a future birth. After all, the cognition at the moment of death in this life is presumably causally efficacious in precisely the same way that the last cognition of the previous life was.

There are various ways to try to block the regress this argument trades upon. One is to invoke the hypothesis of the existence of God. That is, we might argue that the first non-physically caused mental state in the life of an individual was caused by a divine mental state. The individual is not, then, beginningless. Moreover the existence of the consciousness series is thus dependent upon God's existence, i.e. He is the

---

[9] This sort of view can be found in Vasubandhu's *Abhidharmakośa*: compare Karl H. Potter, *Presuppositions of India's Philosophies*, pp.130-137; and Th. Stcherbatsky, *The Central Conception of Buddhism and the Meaning of the Word "Dharma"* (London: Royal Asiatic Society, 1923).

creator. However, the regress will apply in the case of God, for the chain of divine mental states is indeed beginningless (God is eternal).

As a Buddhist Śāntarakṣita is unwilling to admit the theistic hypothesis and elsewhere in his work he argues independently against the existence of God. However, even if the theistic hypothesis can be ruled out on other grounds, there remains another possibility. The theistic hypothesis presupposes the truth of a more general principle: viz. that the first non-physically caused mental state in the life of an individual could have been caused by a mental state of some other individual. But if we admit this principle, then we do not need to insist that it is God's mental states which cause the initial mental states of other individuals. Rather, any individual's mental states could cause another's initial mental state. Thus what the regress will now show is the beginninglessness of causally efficient mental states, not the beginninglessness of any particular chain of such states. That is, the existence of conscious beings (conceived of here as causal series) could well be beginningless without this necessitating that any particular conscious being is beginningless. To block this possibility Śāntarakṣita would have to deny the general principle that a person's initial mental state could be directly caused by the mental state of another. Now there seems no *logical* difficulty with such a possibility: telepathy is presumably a putative example of such a phenomenon and that seems at least a coherent hypothesis. Hence the principle will have to be rejected on empirical grounds. That is, it will be maintained that while such causal interactions may be logically possible, it is contingently the case that no such interactions take place in our world. The plausibility of this empirical claim will then be as strong as the case against the existence of the relevant parapsychological phenomena. Assuming this to be still an open question, I leave the matter there.

Of course, this doesn't exhaust the range of escape routes from Śāntarakṣita's regress argument. As I have already indicated, the argument rests upon two principles: the principle of universal causation and the mental-cause principle. Hence the denial of one or both of these principles will disarm the argument. Now some would be willing to deny the first principle and maintain that certain events are uncaused. Data from quantum mechanics is sometimes used to support such a position. However the correct interpretation of this data is highly controversial philosophically. At the very least, it is unclear that the instance of uncaused subatomic events (if they indeed occur) would in any way undermine the causal principle construed as a thesis about macroscopic events. If we then assume that mental events are macroscopic events, the regress argument is untouched.

Another way of denying the causal principle is to opt for contra-causal libertarianism and maintain that certain events are indeed uncaused; most importantly, free human actions. This move can then block the regress by maintaining that the first non-physically caused mental event in the life of an individual need not be mentally caused. Instead it could be uncaused, as are all free mental acts. Of course, libertarianism has its own problems. First, it owes us an account of how such uncaused events can be *actions* done under an agent's control. Secondly, if free acts are uncaused events then how can such events be rendered explicable without appealing to causal explanations? Now it may be that libertarianism is able to present a consistent story about these matters. However, I shall assume for the moment that the principle of universal causation is better entrenched than the libertarian view of acts that are uncaused events.

One final point about the principle of universal causation. I formulated the principle of universal causation as the principle that every event has a cause. But it might be objected that Śāntarakṣita's regress argument seems rather to require a principle to the effect that every event has a prior cause. And such a principle is surely false, for a cause and its effect might be simultaneous (as a train's motion is simultaneous with the motion of its carriages that it causes). Now it does seem reasonable to concede that sometimes causes and effects can be contemporaneous; but this admission need not touch Śāntarakṣita's argument. For either the first non-physically caused mental event of this life is caused by a prior mental event, or else it is caused by a contemporaneous mental event. On the first option, of course, we have the regress underway. On the second option, however, we're no better off. For what is the cause of the mental event that is the contemporaneous cause of the first non-physically caused mental event of this life? Given that it isn't physically caused, then its cause must be either a prior mental event, or else another contemporaneous mental event. In the first case we have the infinite temporal regress underway; in the second case we can ask the same question once again about the cause of that contemporaneous cause. So either we have an infinite temporal regress, or (implausibly) we have an infinity of contemporaneous causes and effects at the beginning of the causal series of each person's mental events.

What about the mental-cause principle then? Materialism, of course, denies this principle; so too does epiphenomenalism. Acceptance of the principle apparently commits us either to idealism or to dualism (i.e. interactionist dualism or parallelism). The standard Indian objection to the strong materialist claim that identifies the mental and the physical is a familiar one, resting upon what Western philosophers sometimes parochially call "Leibniz's Law". That is, it is maintained that mental states have properties not shared by physical states and hence cannot be identical with physical states. Unfortunately the objection is inconclusive since it is usually subjective phenomenal properties that are appealed to and Leibniz's Law is notoriously unreliable in intentional contexts. In any case, the Indian materialists (the Cārvākas or Lokāyatas) generally conceded that consciousness possesses properties which seem peculiar to itself. But these properties, it was asserted, are supervenient upon physical states. Consciousness, then, is an emergent characteristic of the physical states formed by combinations of material elements. Just as, for example, the red colour of *pān* is an emergent property of the ingredients (betel, areca nut, lime), none of which is individually red coloured; so too consciousness is an emergent property of the unconscious material elements.

Putting aside for the moment the opaqueness of the whole notion of emergent properties, Śāntarakṣita has a twofold reply to the Lokāyata view. Firstly, he argues that the materialist claim that the mental is always causally dependent upon the physical is not conclusively established. This is because we cannot apply the customary method of agreement and difference to support the existence of such a universal causal law. Thus in the case of other people, we never have direct access to their mental states to establish the necessary positive and negative concomitance. In our own case, on the other hand, although we can observe the concomitance of some mental and bodily states, we obviously cannot do this for the *first* mental event of our present life. Hence there is no proof that the two sets of phenomena are causally related in the way the materialist claims. Secondly, it seems that there is in fact evidence to suggest that some mental states are not totally physically caused. In dreams or imaginings, for example, the mind can apparently work independently of external physical stimuli. Perhaps, then, some mental states could even occur independently of *any* physical cause.

Now the whole question of the relation of the mental and the physical is, of course, a deep and tangled one; one I do not intend to pursue any further here. All I want to claim here and now is that if we concede Śāntarakṣita his mental-cause principle (as many philosophers would) and also his principle of universal causation (as again many philosophers would), then his argument is apparently sound — though, as was pointed out, he has to deny direct causal relations between minds. The argument shows, then, at least the possibility of pre-existence (and with it, rebirth). Indeed, depending upon the strength of one's commitments to the premises of the argument, it can surely make the notion of pre-existence (and rebirth) extremely plausible. This, I take it, should be a surprising conclusion to those Western philosophers who might be sympathetic to the principles that generate Śāntarakṣita's argument.

III

Karl Potter's argument is rather different from Śāntarakṣita's.[10] Whereas Śāntarakṣita's is an argument for the pre-existence of the consciousness series, Potter's is an argument for the beginningless pre-existence of the morally responsible agent. It involves no detailed account of the nature of such a beginningless agent and certainly doesn't involve any overt commitment to dualism or idealism. Nevertheless there is a

---

[10] Karl H. Potter, "Pre-existence" in P. T. Raju and Alburey Castell, eds., *East-West Studies on the Problem of the Self* (The Hague: Martinus Nijhoff, 1968), pp. 193-207. This paper was originally presented in 1965 and Potter briefly reiterates the argument in order to build upon it in his "Freedom and Determinism from an Indian Perspective" *Philosophy East and West* 17 (1967): 113-124 (especially pp. 114-116). The argument has an ancestral connection with one offered in John Wisdom, *Problems of Mind and Matter* (Cambridge: Cambridge University Press, 1934), pp. 123-126.

certain family resemblance between the two arguments at least insofar as both are infinite regress arguments.

Briefly the argument is as follows. Suppose we analyse "A has the ability to ϕ" as roughly something like "A is in a condition such that, given opportunity, if he tries to ϕ then he succeeds a certain percentage of the time".[11] Now consider a particular case: "Smith has the ability to raise-his-arm-at-t_2" will thus be analysed as something like "There is a condition C such that if at t_n Smith is in C and, given opportunity, tries to raise his arm, then he succeeds in raising his arm at t_{n+1} a certain percentage of the time; and Smith is in C at t_1". But if Smith has the ability to raise his arm at t_2 then it must also be true that he has the ability to try to raise his arm at t_1. However, trying to raise his arm is itself another action and hence Smith's ability to perform this action is open to a parallel analysis to that given to "Smith has the ability to raise-his-arm-at-t_2". That is: "There is a condition C' such that if at t_{n-1} Smith is in C' and, given opportunity, tries to try-at-t_n-to-raise-his-arm-at-t_{n+1}, then he succeeds in trying-at-t_n-to-raise-his-arm-at-t_{n+1} a certain percentage of the time; and Smith is in C' at t_0".

Obviously we can now generate a regress. Moreover, given that Smith's responsibility for raising his arm requires that he has the ability to raise his arm, then his responsibility for trying to raise his arm requires that he has the ability to try to raise his arm. Thus if the ability to try to ϕ is a prerequisite for attributing responsibility to someone for ϕ-ing, the agent must be beginningless. Otherwise there is some action of the agent which he is unable to try to perform and yet his ability to perform it is a necessary condition of his being responsible for his performance of ϕ. That is, if the agent is not beginningless he cannot be responsible for any of his actions.

Note that the argument is for the thesis that the agent must have the ability to perform an infinite number of actions in order to perform any action at all. But the analysis does not require that an action must be preceded by another action; only that an action must be preceded by the agent's *ability* to perform another action. In other words, the regress involved here is not the regress that the notion of basic actions is supposed to block. What the argument is supposed to show, then, is that an agent can

---

[11] Such an analysis is offered in Arnold S. Kaufman, "Ability" *Journal of Philosophy* **60** (1963): 537-551.

never come into existence, but must have existed beginninglessly. For suppose that there was a first event in an agent's history. In that case that first event is not an action since there is no prior condition the agent was in (as required by the analysis of "having the ability to act" assumed here). But then neither can any subsequent event be an action of that agent either, for no subsequent event could be preceded by the appropriate conditions. Thus the agent never acts, or has always had the ability to act. If the agent is acting now, he must be beginningless.

Naturally some will be disposed to regard this conclusion as a *reductio* of the presupposed analysis of ability or of the sort of account of responsibility that utilizes it. However, it does seem that a similar argument could be generated from any conditional analysis of ability. That is, any analysis that explicates ability in terms of a subjunctive conditional of some form.[12] Of course, the critic might also welcome this more general conclusion, in which case he presumably owes us an alternative and superior account of ability. Be that as it may, there does remain one possible attempt to avoid the conclusion of the regress argument while accepting the general sort of account of ability. The argument, it will be remembered, assumes that having the ability is causally relevant to an agent's performing an action. The regress then generated presupposes that the ability to perform the act involves the existence of a condition of the agent prior to the performance of the act. But this surely need not be the case. For given that the idea is that the appropriate condition is causally relevant, then (as we earlier remarked) a cause need not temporally precede its effect; it might be contemporaneous with its effect. Could, then, an ability to perform an action come into existence contemporaneously with the performance of the action? And would this prevent the regress argument that implies the beginninglessness of the agent?

It seems that there is such an escape route, though how attractive it would be is unclear. Let's suppose there is an event *E* which is the first event in an agent's history. For that event to be an action performed by the agent there would also have to be another event *E'*, the agent's ability to try to bring about *E*. (This will be an event insofar as, on the account of ability assumed here, it involves the occurrence of an

---

[12] On such analyses and their difficulties see Lawrence H. Davis, *Theory of Action* (Englewood Cliffs, N. J.: Prentice-Hall, 1979), Ch. 3.

appropriate condition of the agent.) And this in turn means that there must be a third event E'' (the agent's ability to try to try to bring about E) — and so on. But now suppose that we allow E, E', E'' etc. to be all contemporaneous. In this case we can then avoid the temporal regress to the beginninglessness of the agent. However, if we do this then we have to accept that the first action which the agent performed involved the simultaneous occurrence of an infinite number of causally implicated contemporaneous events. (Not all of these events, of course, are other actions.) Hence the regress that implies the beginninglessness of the agent can be evaded in this way, but at a cost. One consequence of this escape route is that the agent's performance of his first action also supposedly involves the simultaneous occurrence of an infinity of other contemporaneous events, all of which are causally implicated in the occurrence of that first action.[13] It is hard to see that this is much more plausible than the beginninglessness of the agent.

Anyway, rather than press the matter any further here let's look instead at exactly what the argument would establish if it were indeed sound. The thesis it purports to establish is the beginninglessness of an agent. By itself, however, this thesis entails no detailed theory about the number or nature of such agents. Nevertheless an important point about Indian views of rebirth is brought out by the argument. For (as Potter points out) it is the active factors of personality that all Indian philosophers regard as that which has beginningless existence; i.e. our powers of choice and discrimination, our abilities. Hence I propose a minimal account of the beginningless agent by characterizing an agent as a locus of (basic) actions and abilities.[14] Such a definition seems required both philosophically and exegetically. Philosophically it is necessary to identify the agent with the locus of actions and abilities if we are to avoid the problem of how otherwise to connect an agent and her abilities on the one side with

---

[13] A similar difficulty for Chisholm's account of agent causalism is pointed out in Graham Oddie, "Control" in R. G. Durrant, ed., *Essays in Honour of Gwen Taylor*, pp. 198-199.

[14] Cf. the suggestion in Arthur C. Danto, *Analytical Philosophy of Action* (Cambridge: Cambridge University Press, 1973) that the limits of my self are defined by my repertoire of basic actions. Danto, however, identifies basic actions with physiological processes and hence identifies agents with their bodily processes. The account I am proposing is neutral with regard to the question of whether there are irreducibly mental basic acts.

her actions on the other. Between an agent and her basic actions there is no gap to bridge. Exegetically the proposal accords well with the doctrine of karma, a doctrine crucially intertwined with the Indian belief in rebirth. This is the doctrine that our actions have causal consequences which determine our subsequent situations. Thus my present circumstances are the effect of my previous deeds, just as my future circumstances will be determined by my present actions. (The term "karma" derives from the Sanskrit root "*kṛ*", to act.)

Consider in this regard the following passage from the *Bṛhadāraṇyaka Upaniṣad* (IV.4.5):

> According as one acts, according as one conducts himself, so does he become. The doer of good becomes good. The doer of evil becomes evil. One becomes virtuous by virtuous action, bad by bad action.
>
> But people say: "A person is made [not of acts, but] of desires only." [In reply to this I say:] As is his desire, such is his resolve; as is his resolve, such the action he performs; what action (*karma*) he performs, [into that does he become changed].[15]

The first part of this quotation, of course, is a succinct statement of the doctrine of karma. However, at the same time it is highly suggestive for our purposes in that it apparently identifies the agent with his actions. Then, in reply to an objection, it broadens this account to include the causal components of his actions, i.e. his desires and resolutions (or perhaps "volitions" since the Sanskrit "*kratuḥ*" may be translated as "will" as well as "resolve"). This surely amounts to much the same as the suggestion that an agent is the locus of basic actions and abilities (insofar as these latter are causal components of his basic actions).

It might seem simpler here to drop the use of the term "locus" and simply identify the agent with the set of his actions, or even just with the set of desires that

---

[15] *The Thirteen Principal Upanishads*, trans, Robert Ernest Hume, 2nd rev. ed. (London: Oxford University Press, 1931), p. 140.

cause the actions.[16] However, there are two objections to such a proposal: one philosophical and one exegetical. The philosophical objection is that it is unclear how we are to individuate agents on such an account. For it seems possible that there could be two exactly similar desire-sets characterizing two distinct agents. And yet on this account such agents would have to be identical. The exegetical objection is that such an account is too nominalistic to be an acceptable exposition of the general Indian view. Desires and actions are apparently properties of an agent, and many Indian philosophers wish to insist upon a distinction between properties and property-possessors.

My use of the term "locus" was suggested by the Sanskrit philosophical terms "*āśraya*" and "*adhiṣṭhāna*", both of which are often translated as "locus". Roughly speaking, in Indian philosophy an *āśraya* or *adhiṣṭhāna* is that which things reside "in" or "on" or "at". It is not necessarily conceived of as spatio-temporal; (it certainly isn't so conceived in Nyāya-Vaiśeṣika, for example). However, spatio-temporal difference implies difference of loci. The locus of a property or object X is that in which X resides. Thus on realist accounts the relation of a property to its locus is the relation of a universal to the particular it characterizes, or the relation between a property and the substance it is "in".

Now in proposing an account of an agent as a locus of basic actions and abilities I have deliberately left open the question of what sort of an account is to be given of the relation between properties and their loci. Hence the minimal definition offered should be unexceptionable to almost all Indian philosophers. Where they differ is in what further account of properties and property-possessors they maintain. Hindu philosophers, for example, tend to favour some sort of realist or conceptualist account which understands the loci to be substances (material or immaterial). On the other hand, nominalist Buddhist philosophers, working with an event ontology, eliminate property-possessors in favour of bundles of properties or property-instances. However, these are further metaphysical questions which need not prevent all of these philosophers agreeing that an agent is a locus of basic actions and abilities.

---

[16] For the suggestion that the self is simply a set of actual or potential desires (needs, wants, and interests) see Herman, pp. 192-195.

But even if the exegetical problem is met by my account, what about the individuation problem? There certainly is a philosophical problem here. However, this is not a particular problem for the proposed account of an agent. It is just a special case of a general metaphysical problem about properties and property-possessors. If we understand loci to be substantial property-possessors then we have to be able to individuate substances. But if an agent is a substance, then how do we individuate substances as distinct from the properties they possess? On the other hand, if we reject substances as the Buddhists do, then there are no individuals to be identified as agents but only causally related patterns of events. Agents (like all "entities") are analysed as processes, patterns of events. But then the problem is how to individuate such processes. Either way, there is no special problem about the individuation of agents. Whatever general metaphysical account is to be given of the relation of a property to its locus will be used to deal with the individuation problem about agents. Similarly, whatever general account is given of identity preservation through change of properties will also be used to deal with the problem of what preserves identity of the agent through time and change (including rebirth). On these general metaphysical questions Indian philosophers (like their Western counterparts) take various positions so that it cannot be said that there is one general Indian account of these matters.

IV

The obvious objection at this point is that even if we can concede the metaphysical coherence of the notion of a beginningless agent conceived of as a locus of basic actions and abilities, yet such a concept of an agent is clearly not identical with the concept of a person. Hence pre-existence and rebirth so conceived do not really involve any sort of personal continuance. And this, of course, is true insofar as it goes. Indeed it is precisely what we would expect, given any knowledge of the Indian context of the doctrine of rebirth. Thus it is part of the Indian view that we can be reborn not just as humans, but as gods, demons, animals and even plants. It is hard to see that any account of *personal* identity could embrace such successive rebirths. Moreover, the Indian religio-philosophical tradition is deeply opposed to a concern with what most Westerners would consider ordinary human personality, regarding such a concern as a source of bondage to suffering. The eschatologies of Indian religions generally present a picture of final release wherein the agent so blessed is a very different sort of being from our ordinary conception of a person. And this in turn is one instance of the radically different conception of the nature and value of the individual person in Indian thought as compared with that familiar to us from, for example, the Judaeo-Christian tradition.

However, these remarks just seem to invite further objections. At least three questions naturally come to mind. Firstly, if there is no sense of strong personal identity across lives, then surely the theory is entirely void of any genuine personal significance? Secondly, if my rebirth is not the same person as me, then why should I concern myself with his fate? Thirdly, if he is not the same person as me, then how can he justly incur the karmic consequences of *my* actions (as the doctrine of karma maintains).[17]

The first problem, then, is whether the doctrine of rebirth is essentially vacuous in personal terms, even though it might be a metaphysical possibility. In this connection consider, for instance, the argument from the fact that we do not normally remember our putative previous lives. Now clearly the truth of this claim cannot in itself rule out the possibility of our pre-existence: I do not remember what I ate for lunch three weeks ago, but this does not entail that I didn't have lunch then. Rather, the point seems to be that in the absence of memory the past lives would form only a disconnected series with no sense of personal continuity between them. The connections between lives would then be too weak to make the idea of rebirth of any real interest personally. In his *Discourse on Metaphysics* (sect.34) Leibniz put the point thus:

> Suppose that some individual could suddenly become King of China on condition, however, of forgetting what he had been, as though being born again, would it not amount to the same practically, or as far as the effects could be perceived, as if the individual were annihilated, and a King of

---

[17] For an interesting discussion of these sorts of objections in relation to Theravāda Buddhism see Peter Forrest, "Reincarnation Without Survival of Memory or Character" *Philosophy East and West* **28** (1978): 91-97.

China were the same instant created in his place? The individual would have no reason to desire this.[18]

In reply to this argument we might begin by pointing out that there is at least one sense of memory which is not explicitly excluded in Leibniz's scenario. For example, I remember how to tie shoelaces without remembering when and where I learnt to do this. Thus it is possible that memories as abilities or capacities might link lives in a fashion that is of some personal relevance without there being conscious memories of the experiences of these previous lives. And in fact the doctrine of karma does maintain that certain dispositions of the sort alluded to here carry across lives. The second point that needs to be made is that some people do claim to remember their previous lives. In the Indian tradition such an ability is thought to be typical of saints and *yogins*. (The Buddhist tradition, for instance, very early linked the acquisition of the ability to recall former births with the actual enlightenment experience of Gautama Buddha.)[19] Moreover, claimed memories of former lives are by no means limited to saints. Occasionally even ordinary people maintain that they have memories of at least fragments of previous lives; such memories including subsequently confirmed data which would seem to have not been available to them in any usual way.[20] Although such cases may not be frequent and well documented enough to be conclusive evidence for rebirth, they are nevertheless strongly suggestive of rebirth. Furthermore, they serve to undermine the claim that the rebirth doctrine is entirely vacuous in personal terms.

These remarks, however, are inconclusive as they stand. In the first place, while it is surely possible that certain dispositions can carry across lives (our genetic

---

[18] *Leibniz Selections*, ed. Philip P. Wiener (New York: Charles Scribner's Sons, 1951), p. 340.

[19] See, for instance, *Majjhima Nikāya* I.248 and *Saṃyutta Nikāya* II.213. There are numerous other references in the Pali Canon to the ability of an adept to recall past lives: see *Dīgha Nikāya* I.81; *Majjhima Nikāya* I. 482, II.31, III.99 etc..

[20] On such cases the careful researches of Professor Ian Stevenson should be consulted: see his *The Evidence for Survival from Claimed Memories of Former Incarnations* (Tadworth: M. C. Peto, 1961); *Twenty Cases Suggestive of Reincarnation* 2nd ed. (Charlottesville: University of Virginia Press, 1974); and *Cases of the Reincarnation Type*, Vols. 1-3 (Charlottesville: University of Virginia Press, 1975-79).

inheritance would instance this); yet this degree of psychological continuity may be felt to be too weak to count as *rebirth*. It seems we require some element of memory for the doctrine to have any real personal significance. Of course, the requirement that we actually remember our previous lives is too strong. To preserve the theory from personal vacuity perhaps all we need is the requirement of latent memories. That is, if memory of any given life may be regained at some later point in the series of lives, then this possibility will provide sufficient continuity to hold the series together and hence guarantee the non-vacuity of the concept.[21]

But this suggestion is likely to be judged unsatisfactory for the following reason. The thesis is that the psychological continuity required to make the notion of rebirth non-vacuous can be explicated in terms of actual or latent memories. There is, however, an obvious and fundamental difference between *really* remembering and *seeming* to remember. I can only have real memories of my previous life if I am the same person as the person whose life I remember. But the account of rebirth under discussion supposedly does not insist that I am in any strong sense the *same person* as the person whose life I remember and whom I claim to be a rebirth of.

To meet this objection we need to prise memories (latent or otherwise) away from actual past experiences of those who remember. This can be done by taking over a suggestion of Derek Parfit's and introducing a new notion of memory which he calls "*q*-memory":

> I am *q*-remembering an experience if (1) I have a belief about a past experience which seems in itself like a memory belief, (2) someone did have such an experience, and (3) my belief is dependent upon this experience in the same way (whatever that is) in which a memory of an experience is dependent upon it.[22]

Memories, then, are just *q*-memories of one's own experiences. The concept of *q*-memories is the wider concept; the class of memories is a subset of the class of *q*-

---

[21] Cf. C. J. Ducasse, *A Critical Examination of the Belief in a Life After Death* (Springfield, Ill.: Charles C. Thomas, 1961), p. 225.

[22] Derek Parfit, "Personal Identity", p. 15.

memories. If we drop the narrower concept of memory in favour of the wider concept of q-memory, then we can explicate the memory condition that provides the psychological continuity across the series of lives in terms of latent q-memory. The account so modified is not then open to the objection that it requires a stronger sense of personal identity than it is willing to admit.

The view outlined so far, then, does provide for a sense of continuity which would guarantee the non-vacuity of the doctrine of rebirth in personal terms without insisting upon strict identity across lives. This seems to capture the general Indian view. In the Buddhist tradition, for example, this view is expressed by the claim that the reborn person is "neither the same nor another" (*na ca so na ca añño*) in relation to the deceased whose karma he inherits. Thus the well known exchange in the *Milinda-pañha* (II,2,1):

> The king asked: "When someone is reborn, Venerable Nagasena, is he the same as the one who just died, or is he another?" — The Elder replied: "He is neither the same nor another".[23]

Insofar, however, as the reborn person is the karmic heir of the deceased, linked to him or her by both causally induced dispositions and latent q-memories, it is appropriate to regard them as the same agent, even if they are not strictly the same person.[24]

V

Two further objections to the theory of rebirth were mentioned earlier. They can be conveniently grouped together in that they both concern the moral dimensions of the theory. The first is expressed in the question: "If my rebirth is not strictly speaking

---

[23] Edward Conze, *Buddhist Scriptures* (Harmondsworth: Penguin, 1959), pp. 149-150.

[24] Cf. *Mahābhārata* XII 218.35 where there is a criticism (apparently directed at the Buddhist view) of the idea that karma should fall to the lot of other than the doer of the deed. Of course, the Buddhist would concede this but deny that "same doer or agent" is equivalent to "same person". Moreover, he would point out that his Hindu opponents must also admit this non-equivalence. Where they differ is on the question of whether "*a* is the same (agent) as *b*" involves absolute or only relative identity.

the same person as myself, then why should I concern myself with his fate?" The answer is that there is a moral obligation towards one's karmic heir. Not only is there a general presumption that we are morally obliged to consider the interests of future generations, but there is a self-referentially altruistic argument for particularly concerning oneself with the fate of one's karmic heir. For it is generally felt that one has a particular obligation to those closest to oneself (relatives, friends etc.) and on this theory one's karmic heir is the very closest of surviving relations. Moreover, if we assume that people are most easily motivated by egoistic concerns, then the more closely we identify with our karmic heirs, the easier it will be to fulfil our moral responsibilities to them. Hence regarding one's karmic heir as the closest moral equivalent to oneself will make it easier to fulfil one's moral obligations.

The other objection, it will be recalled, was to do with the apparent injustice of someone not identical with me incurring the karmic consequences of *my* actions. Strictly speaking, this is not an objection to the theory of rebirth but to the doctrine of karma. However, since the two doctrines are closely intertwined in the Indian tradition, it is appropriate to say something about this charge. In the first place the objection presupposes the truth of a retributivist account of just punishment. That is, it is assumed that it is only just for me to suffer the karmic consequences of a person's actions if I am that very same person. But on alternative deterrence or reformative theories of punishment it may be justifiable in certain circumstances to punish some-one for an action he did not commit. Secondly, if we conceive of the "law of karma" as involving the claim that "justice is done", then what we have is an implicit theory of justice according to which one's responsibility for actions does not necessarily involve one's strict identity with the person who performed these actions. That is, "x is right to hold y responsible" is the primitive relation and "A has the karma of having done b" entails "A is rightly held responsible for having done b".[25] Such a theory may seem more plausible if we recall that it is certainly a psychological fact that people can feel responsible or be held by others to be responsible for deeds not committed by them. Thus the guilt of some whites over their ancestors' treatment of black slaves, or the way in which some blacks hold all whites to be responsible for past mistreatments of

---

[25] Cf. Forrest, p. 94.

blacks. (This example is, of course, only supposed to show that the idea that one person can be responsible for the actions of another person isn't so alien a notion as all that. It is not claimed that this proves that such ascriptions are in fact just.)

Finally, it is sometimes objected that the moral intelligibility of the doctrine that my present circumstances are the result of actions in a previous life requires that we remember such lives. Otherwise there can be no sense in which someone can be held responsible for an action of which she knows nothing and which occurred before she was born. Hick suggests that this argument can be met by invoking the possibility of latent memories which at some later time are recovered and hence link together the series of lives and deeds in a morally intelligible way.[26] However, even without appealing to Hick's rejoinder, the objection surely won't do. Suppose that as the result of an accident caused by himself a man both kills a pedestrian and also incurs amnesia so that he can remember neither the accident nor the circumstances leading to it. His responsibility for the accident is certainly not diminished by his present circumstances. Nor need he *remember* his actions to feel responsible; all he needs for that is the *belief* that he was responsible for the accident. Thus neither responsibility nor the feeling of being responsible require memory (latent or actual).

VI

To conclude then. I have argued for the metaphysical coherence of the general Indian account of rebirth. To this end two arguments for pre-existence were considered. The first of these was for the pre-existence (and, by analogy, post-existence) of the consciousness series. Given certain qualifications, the argument was found to be sound. The second argument for the pre-existence of the agent was also found to be plausible (given, once again, certain qualifications). However, neither argument

---

[26] *Death and Eternal Life* , p. 354. However, Hick is much more impressed by the argument that the doctrine of karma cannot satisfactorily explain away the problem of suffering (including the inequality of human birth and circumstances) because it involves an infinite regress of explanations which ultimately leaves the phenomenon unexplained: see *Death and Eternal Life*, pp. 308-309 and *Philosophy of Religion*, pp. 141-142. This argument seems to me unsatisfactory, based as it is upon a confusion about the nature of explanation and explanatory ultimates. For criticism see the Appendix.

establishes the pre-existence or post-existence of *persons* (unless one is unwisely willing simply to identify these with the consciousness series of the first argument). But this is to be expected when we remember the rather different conception of the nature and value of personal existence operating in the Indian context. Nevertheless the notion of the pre-existence and post-existence of the beginningless agent (conceived of as a locus of actions and abilities) was argued to be not only a metaphysically coherent view, but also one which would be non-vacuous in terms of personal significance.

Of course, the Indians consider the doctrine of rebirth to be more than just a metaphysically coherent theory. Typically they regard the existence of the beginning-less cycle of birth, death and rebirth (*saṃsāra*) to be a disagreeable fact. The eschatological goal of the Indian religio-philosophical tradition is complete freedom (*mokṣa*) from this cycle. In keeping with our general account of the agent as a locus of actions and abilities, complete freedom in this tradition is conceived of as a state of non-action wherein those abilities which individuate the agent are nevertheless retained.[27] The agent in such a state doesn't necessarily cease to exist, even though such an agent is no longer aware of himself *as* an individual. Once again the basic conception of the nature and value of personal existence presupposed here is very different from the traditional Western view and hence so too is the treatment of the notion of immortality. Of course, there still remains the philosophical matter of the nature and value of this Indian goal of complete freedom. But that is another question, (though one that I have already discussed some aspects of in Chapters 5 and 6).

---

[27] Cf. Potter, "Pre-existence", p. 205.

POSTSCRIPT

In the Introduction I previewed the overall argument of this work and hence it would be tedious by way of conclusion simply to summarize once again what was said there. However perhaps it is nevertheless worth briefly highlighting the main themes that have emerged in the course of the investigation. Four in particular seem to me to stand out: three of these concern the substantive philosophical problems I have discussed in the bulk of this work and the fourth is methodological. Together they constitute the main strands of the inquiry. Let me begin, then, with the three themes related to the primary philosophical issues about death and immortality. First, I considered in Chapters 1 and 2 the notion of death in both its subjective and objective dimensions and offered an account of death that is neutral with respect to the possibility of postmortem survival. Second, in Chapters 3 and 4 I discussed the relation of death to the meaning and value of life, including the matter of how best to live rationally in the face of death. This involved consideration both of the question of the reasonableness of the fear of death and of the problem of how to live, as Tolstoy puts it, "so that death cannot destroy life". Third, in Chapters 5-8 I addressed the notion of immortality, both the value of such a possibility and its metaphysical coherence. Although I was sceptical about the value of immortality, I was much less sceptical than is perhaps nowadays common about the philosophical coherence of traditional eschatologies like disembodied existence, resurrection and rebirth. However in each case I was careful to indicate that there are metaphysical and ethical costs to be counted. (For example, in order to make plausible such views it seems to be necessary to countenance a weaker sense of personal identity than has been generally recognized — at least in Western philosophy.)

This sort of concern with indicating the philosophical costs of a position is the fourth, methodological theme. It is, of course, a general feature of the methodology of this work; as I believe it is of much philosophical inquiry. It is very rare in philosophy to be able to provide knock-down arguments, particularly in areas like metaphysics, ethics and philosophy of religion. Rather the usual procedure is to try to tease out the full implications of a position and clarify exactly what its costs are. Whether someone is willing to pay those costs will be up to that person and the reasonableness of the decision has to be judged holistically in terms of criteria like the overall coherence and explanatory power of the implied system of beliefs when compared with rival systems. This does not mean that I take no stands on these issues; on the contrary, I have argued for a number of controversial philosophical theses. But I recognize that the plausibility of these arguments and theses depends in turn upon the plausibility of other controversial arguments and theses — a point I have taken some pains to emphasize in the course of this inquiry. This feature of philosophical investigation makes it a characteristically open-ended activity as proposed solutions to philosophical difficulties typically raise in turn yet other problems to be considered. Nevertheless it would be a mistake to imagine that nothing has been achieved just because at the conclusion of this inquiry other philosophical questions still remain to be answered. It is not just that, obviously enough, not everything can be done in a single work. Rather there is a deeper sense in which this open-endedness is somehow constitutive of successful philosophical activity. And here I can do no better than to recall Wittgenstein's remark in the *Philosophical Investigations* (sect. 133):

> The real discovery is the one that makes me capable of stopping doing phil-
> osophy when I want to. — The one that gives philosophy peace, so that it is
> no longer tormented by questions which bring *itself* in question. — Instead,
> we now demonstrate a method, by examples; and the series of examples can
> be broken off.—Problems are solved (difficulties eliminated), not a *single*
> problem.

APPENDIX

KARMA AND THE PROBLEM OF SUFFERING

Earlier (p. 169) I referred to an objection raised by John Hick against the viability of the theory of karma as a solution to the problem of suffering (including the inequality of human birth and circumstances). Of course, the theory of karma is logically distinct from the doctrine of rebirth and hence such questions of karma are arguably outside the compass of our earlier inquiry into the metaphysical coherence of the doctrine of rebirth. However, karma and rebirth are doctrines so closely intertwined in the Indian tradition that I feel it is nevertheless appropriate to include here as an appendix to our earlier discussion a more elaborate consideration of this question of karma and the problem of suffering.

Although the concept of karma is well known to be fundamental to Indian religious thought, it is still rare to find an analytic philosopher of religion willing to engage seriously this (or any other) Indian religious notion. One laudable exception to this parochial trend is to be found in the recent writings of John Hick, whose excellent introductory work *Philosophy of Religion* now includes a discussion of Indian conceptions of karma and rebirth.[1] Nevertheless it seems to me that his account there of the adequacy of the doctrine of karma as a solution to the problem of suffering is unsatisfactory.

The efficacy of the doctrine of karma as a solution to the problem of suffering has often been espoused, both in India and in the West. Thus Max Weber, for instance, regarded it as "the most consistent theodicy ever produced by history."[2] (Note that Weber uses the term "theodicy" here to refer to an attempt to answer the general existential need to explain suffering and evil, rather than just the resolution of a prima facie conflict between the existence of suffering and God's alleged omnipotence and

---

[1] John Hick, *Philosophy of Religion*, 3rd ed., Ch. 10. This material first appeared in Chapter 8 of the second edition of the book (1973).

[2] Max Weber, *The Religion of India* (New York: The Free Press, 1958), p. 121.

benevolence.)[3] Now Hick is quite aware of this sort of claim. Indeed he suggests that one of the reasons why the Indians believe in karma and reincarnation is that the hypothesis "makes sense of many aspects of human life, including the inequalities of human birth" (p. 140). However Hick himself refuses to admit that the doctrine provides a viable theodicy (in the Weberian sense):

> Either there is a first life, characterized by initial human differences, or else (as in the Vedāntic philosophy) there is no first life but a beginningless series of incarnations. In the latter case the explanation of the inequalities of our present life is endlessly postponed and never achieved, for we are no nearer to an ultimate explanation of the circumstances of our present birth when we are told that they are the consequences of a previous life, if that previous life has in turn to be explained by reference to a yet previous life, and that by reference to another, and so on, in an infinite regress. One can affirm the beginningless character of the soul's existence in this way, but one cannot then claim that it renders either intelligible or morally acceptable the inequalities found in our present human lot. The solution has not been produced but only postponed to infinity (pp. 141-142).[4]

Now this surely won't do. What is the problem of suffering that is being posed here? Is it the problem of explaining the inequalities of any given person's present life? Well, then the doctrine of karma explains my present situation by reference to the causal influences of the deeds of my previous life. Of course, it is conceded that my previous life situation is to be explained by reference to my life before that, and so on. It is also true that the Indians believe this cycle of rebirths to be beginningless (anādi)

---

[3] Max Weber, *The Sociology of Religion* (Boston: Beacon Press, 1963), Ch. 9. On this usage compare Gananath Obeyesekere, "Theodicy, Sin and Salvation in a Sociology of Buddhism" in E. R. Leach, ed., *Dialectic in Practical Religion* (Cambridge: Cambridge University Press, 1968), pp. 7-40. On the relevance of the hypothesis of rebirth and karma to the latter, narrower sense of "theodicy" see Arthur L. Herman, *The Problem of Evil and Indian Thought.*

[4] The same objection is urged in Hick's *Death and Eternal Life*, pp. 308-309.

and thus there is an infinite regress here.[5] But it is not a vicious one, for there is no particular instance of suffering that is inexplicable. (Classical Indian philosophers were well aware of the distinction between a vicious and a non-vicious infinite regress. Their stock example of the latter is the case of the seed and the sprout: the seed which produces the sprout is a different seed from the one produced by the sprout, and so this is merely a beginningless causal series.)

Compare in this regard the problem of explaining my existence. I might offer an account in terms of certain deeds of my parents that resulted in my conception. Of course, the existence of my parents would have to be explained in terms of similar deeds of my grandparents, and the existence of my grandparents in terms of my great-grandparents, and so on. But, notwithstanding the possibility of this chain being infinitely regressive, when I have offered an explanation of my existence in terms of my parents' conception of me, have I really failed to explain my existence at all?

Thus each particular instance of suffering is, *ex hypothesi*, in principle causally explicable in terms of the prior occurrence of previous deeds of the sufferer. Hence there is no explanatory gap that the theory of karma fails to fill. Now someone might object that though each particular case of suffering in explicable in this way, yet the existence of the whole phenomenon of this beginningless chain of suffering is unexplained. But then the Indians can reply with Hume:

> But the WHOLE, you say, wants a cause. I answer, that the uniting of these parts into a whole, like the uniting of several distinct counties into one kingdom, or several distinct members into one body, is performed merely by an arbitrary act of the mind, and has no influence on the nature of things. Did I show you the particular causes of each individual in a collection of twenty particles of matter, I should think it very unreasonable, should you afterwards ask me, what was the cause of the whole twenty. This is sufficiently explained in explaining the cause of the parts.[6]

---

[5] On the importance of the notion of beginninglessness for Indian philosophy see Fernando Tola and Carmen Dragonetti, *"Anāditva* or Beginninglessness in Indian Philosophy" *Annals of the Bhandarkar Oriental Institute* **61** (1980): 1-20.

[6] David Hume, *Dialogues Concerning Natural Religion*, ed. N. Kemp Smith, pp. 190-191.

But perhaps this is not how Hick conceives of the problem of suffering at all. Maybe the problem of suffering for Hick is not the explanation of the existence of particular cases of suffering. This can indeed be done (at least in principle) by reference to the prior actions of beginningless agents. Rather Hick wants what he calls an "ultimate explanation" of suffering. By this he doesn't mean an explanation of the causal chain of karmic deeds and consequences *as a whole*, thus committing the fallacy of composition. Rather he perhaps wants to say that even if the existence of each contingent instance of suffering can be explained satisfactorily by the prior existence of the contingent deeds of the sufferer, the question "Why is there suffering at all?" arises. The existence of suffering in our world is a contingent fact about this world; there are possible worlds in which there is no suffering. If it is to be explicable at all it cannot be explained in terms of other contingent facts about the deeds of the sufferers. This is what is meant by the demand for an "ultimate explanation" of suffering.

Now the Indian answer to this will be that, while individual instances of suffering are explicable by reference to karma, the fact that suffering exists in our world at all (given that there are possible worlds in which it does not) is just a brute fact about our world. And this reply seems perfectly reasonable. Explanation has to come to an end somewhere; there have to be some brute facts. The counter-claim that suffering is thus ultimately unintelligible is just an emotionally coloured response to the inevitable way that explanatory chains terminate.[7] The "ultimate explanation" that is being asked for just doesn't exist and to persist in demanding it is just to misunderstand the nature of explanation.

That this is so can be highlighted by consideration of a possible attempt to provide such an "ultimate explanation". Suppose we explain the existence of suffering in relation to God's purposes. We espouse, in other words, some sort of "soul-making" theodicy such that the existence of the contingent fact of suffering is explained by reference to its being required by God's plans for us to develop morally as free persons, evolving eventually into "children of God". (Hick himself, of course,

---

[7] Cf. M. O'C. Drury, *The Danger of Words* (London: Routledge & Kegan Paul, 1973), p. xi: "Do you think there *must* be a significance, an explanation? As I see it there are two sorts of people: one man sees a bird sitting on a telegraph wire and says to himself: 'Why is that bird sitting just there?', the other man replies 'Damn it all, the bird has to sit somewhere'."

espouses a similar theodicy.) Now let's concede *per argumentum* that this both explains in some way the contingent fact of suffering and morally justifies it. But is it an "ultimate explanation" of suffering? Hasn't the contingent existence of suffering just been explained by the contingent fact of God's existence? Why does God exist? After all, He might not have. True, God is held to be a "necessary being". But that can mean either (i) that God is a *logically* necessary being; or (ii) that God is a *factually* necessary being. The first option, however, is incoherent, so any explanation of the fact of suffering in terms of a *logically* necessary being is completely unsatisfactory. The second option is coherent but only means that *if* God exists, then He exists eternally and His existence is not dependent on any other being. However, whether God exists or not is still a contingent matter; there are possible worlds in which He does not. Hence if we explain the contingent fact of suffering by reference to God's existence, we have to explain the contingent fact of God's existence by reference to ... Well, what? Not more contingent facts which themselves require explanation, and so on *ad infinitum*, for then it will be complained (as Hick does of karma) that the explanation "has not been produced but only postponed to infinity." On the other hand, if we terminate our explanation with the contingent fact of God's existence then we are insisting that God's existence is just a brute fact. But now it must be that either (i) appeal to brute facts is perfectly in order in explanation; or (ii) God's existence is ultimately unintelligible and hence so too is the fact of suffering that His existence was supposed to explain.

The trouble with adhering to the second option is that it makes everything "ultimately unintelligible", for we have no idea of what an ultimate explanation of this sort would even look like. This strongly suggests that this is far too stringent a conception of explanation. Explanation as we customarily understand it (paradigmatically, of course, in science) doesn't require anything so grand. True, for explanatory purposes we will take certain things to be just brute facts. But that doesn't mean that explanation by reference to these facts (e.g. that these are the laws of nature that obtain, though there might have been another set) isn't really *explanation*. Thus the explanation of individual sufferings by reference to the theory of karma would indeed (if true) be a satisfactory explanation and hence an adequate theodicy in the Weberian sense.

It will be obvious by now that the pattern of argumentation that I have been outlining is a replication of a familiar debate about the soundness of the cosmological argument for the existence of God. (Thus illustrating Hick's claim (p. 4) that it is "important to see how contemporary philosophical methods can be applied to the ideas of quite different religious traditions.") One version of the cosmological argument (the First-Cause argument) is vitiated by its inability to exclude an infinite regress of causes requiring no beginning. A second version of the argument (the contingency argument) claims that the regress excluded by the argument is a regress of *explanations*, not of events. Thus either (i) the regress of explanations goes back infinitely and there is no ultimate explanation of reality; or (ii) underpinning it all is a self-explanatory reality. The curious point is that Hick himself discussing the cosmological argument in *Philosophy of Religion* (pp. 20-23) admits that the dilemma here is an inconclusive one.[8] The sceptic will take the first horn and admit that the existence of the universe is just a brute fact. It is the theist's inability to exclude this possibility that undermines the power of the cosmological argument as a proof of God's existence. Hick, of course, thinks that this sceptical manœuvre means admitting the universe to be "ultimately unintelligible"; a position he allows, nevertheless, to be logically unassailable. But the sceptic need not concede even this description of his position. He can, after all, in principle explain any event in the universe; the "ultimate explanation" which it is claimed he fails to provide is just, he might well say, a chimera. Nothing can be "ultimately explained", but this doesn't mean nothing can be explained.

The relevance of this to the problem of suffering is clear enough. If the problem of suffering is how to explain particular instances of suffering, then the theory of karma will do this all right by referring to the causal efficacy of the sufferer's previous deeds. (Whether the theory is true is, of course, another matter.) However, if the problem of suffering is to give an "ultimate explanation" of why there is suffering at all, then the theory of karma won't do this. The existence of suffering is just a brute fact about the world. But what sort of "explanation" is being asked for here? How could anything be explicable in this "ultimate" sense? Any proffered explanatory

---

[8] For a fuller account of Hick's views on the cosmological argument see his *Arguments for the Existence of God* (London: Macmillan, 1970), Ch. 3.

candidate would itself be in need of ultimate explanation. If this regress is held to be a vicious one, then surely the conclusion to be drawn is that this is a *reductio ad absurdum* of an over-stringent conception of explanation.

One final point. Throughout I have only been concerned with the *cognitive* problem of suffering, i.e. how to explain why individual (and apparently unmerited) suffering occurs. I have argued that the theory of karma (if true) explains this. But there is also a *psychological* problem of suffering, i.e. how to provide the assurance of comfort, or perhaps ultimate termination of suffering. Of course, the central concern of Indian religions is with the quest for liberation from suffering (*moksa*). But whether the karma theory can meet the psychological problem of suffering is a separate question. In the Hindu tradition, for example, the Vedic and Purāṇic texts evidence a plethora of diverse answers to the problem of the origins of evil, presupposing and yet transcending the logically satisfactory answer offered by the doctrine of karma.[9] It might seem, then, that the Indians themselves are not totally satisfied that karma will solve the psychological problem of suffering. But this is a different matter and does not affect what I have said so far with regard to the adequacy of the doctrine of karma as a solution to the cognitive problem of suffering.

---

[9] Cf. Wendy Doniger O'Flaherty, *The Origins of Evil in Hindu Mythology* (Berkeley: University of California Press, 1976).

SELECTED BIBLIOGRAPHY

Aldwinckle, Russell. *Death in the Secular City*. London: George Allen & Unwin, 1972.

Anselm, Saint. *Anselm of Canterbury, Volume One* , ed. & trans. Jasper Hopkins and Herbert Richardson. London: SCM Press, 1974.

Ariès, Phillipe. *Western Attitudes Toward Death: From the Middle Ages to the Present*. Baltimore: John Hopkins University Press, 1974.

Aristotle. *Ethics*, trans. J. A. K. Thomson. Harmondsworth: Penguin, 1953.

Augustine, Saint. *The City of God*. 2 vols., trans. John Healey. London: J. M. Dent, 1945.

Augustine, Saint. *The Enchiridion of Augustine*. London: Religious Tract Society, n.d.

Badham, Paul. *Christian Beliefs About Life After Death*. London: Macmillan, 1976.

Badham, Paul and Linda. *Immortality or Extinction?* London: Macmillan, 1982.

Baillie, John. *The Idea of Revelation in Recent Thought*. New York: Columbia University Press, 1956.

Beauchamp, Tom L. and Perlin, Seymour. eds. *Ethical Issues in Death and Dying*. Englewood Cliffs, N.J.: Prentice-Hall, 1978.

Becker, Lawrence C.. "Human Being: The Boundaries of the Concept." *Philosophy and Public Affairs* 4 (1975): 334-359.

Black, Henry Campbell. *Black's Law Dictionary*. rev. 4th ed. St. Paul, Minnesota: West, 1968.

Black, Henry Campbell. *Black's Law Dictionary*. 5th ed. St. Paul, Minnesota: West, 1979.

Black, Peter McL. "Three Definitions of Death." *The Monist* 60 (1977): 136-146.

Brennan, Andrew. "Personal Identity and Personal Survival." *Analysis* **42** (1982): 44-50.

Brennan, Andrew. "Survival." *Synthese* **59** (1984): 339-361.

Broad, C. D. "Certain Features in Moore's Ethical Doctrines." In *The Philosophy of G. E. Moore*, pp. 43-57. Edited by Paul Arthur Schilpp. Evanston: Northwestern University, 1942.

Butler, Joseph. *The Works of Joseph Butler*. Vol. 1, ed. W. E. Gladstone. Oxford: Clarendon Press, 1896.

Čapek, Karel. *The Macropulos Secret*, trans. Paul Selver. London: Robert Holden, 1927.

Chakrabarti, A. "Is Liberation (*Mokṣa*) Pleasant?" *Philosophy East and West* **33** (1983): 167-182.

Cherry, Christopher. "Self, Near-Death and Death." *International Journal for Philosophy of Religion* **16** (1984): 3-11.

Chisholm, Roderick M. "Coming into Being and Passing Away: Can the Metaphysician Help?" In *Philosophical Medical Ethics: Its Nature and Significance*, pp. 169-182. Edited by Stuart F. Spicker & H. Tristram Engelhardt, Jr. Dordrecht: D. Reidel, 1977.

Chisholm, Roderick M. *Person and Object*. London: George Allen & Unwin, 1976.

Choron, Jacques. *Death and Western Thought*. New York: Macmillan, 1963.

Clark, Stephen R. L. "Waking-up: A Neglected Model for the Afterlife." *Inquiry* **26** (1983): 209-230.

Clarke, J. J. "John Hick's Resurrection" *Sophia* **10**(3) (1971): 18-22.

Clarke, Samuel. *The Works 1738*. Vol. 3. New York: Garland, 1978.

Conze, Edward. *Buddhist Scriptures*. Harmondsworth: Penguin, 1959.

Cullman, Oscar. *Immortality of the Soul or Resurrection of the Dead?* London: Epworth, 1958.

Danto, Arthur C. *Analytical Philosophy of Action*. Cambridge: Cambridge University Press, 1973.

Davis, Lawrence H. *Theory of Action*. Englewood Cliffs, N. J.: Prentice-Hall, 1979.

Descartes, René. *The Philosophical Works of Descartes*. Vol. 2, trans. E. S. Haldane & G. R. T. Ross. New York: Dover, 1955.

Deutsch, Eliot. *Advaita Vedānta: A Philosophical Reconstruction*. Honolulu: East-West Center Press, 1969.

Deutsch, Eliot and van Buitenen, J. A. B. eds. *A Source Book of Advaita Vedānta*. Honolulu: University Press of Hawaii, 1971.

Devine, Philip K. *The Ethics of Homicide*. Ithaca: Cornell University Press, 1978.

Dilley, Frank B. "Resurrection and the 'Replica Objection'." *Religious Studies* **19** (1983): 459-474.

Donnelly, John. ed. *Language, Metaphysics, and Death*. New York: Fordham University Press, 1978.

Drury, M. O'C. *The Danger of Words*. London: Routledge & Kegan Paul, 1973.

Ducasse, C. J. *A Critical Examination of the Belief in a Life After Death*. Springfield, Ill.: Charles C. Thomas, 1961.

Durrant, R. G. "Identity of Properties and the Definition of 'Good'." *Australasian Journal of Philosophy* **48** (1970): 360-361.

Durrant, R. G. (Bob). "Is Egoism a Possible Morality?" In *Essays in Honour of Gwen Taylor*, pp. 36-51. Edited by R. G. Durrant. Dunedin: Philosophy Department, University of Otago.

Edwards, Paul. *Heidegger on Death: A Critical Evaluation*. La Salle: Hegeler Institute, 1979.

Edwards, Paul. "'My Death'." In *The Encyclopedia of Philosophy*. Vol. 5, pp. 416-419. Edited by Paul Edwards. New York: Macmillan, 1967.

Enright, D. J. ed. *The Oxford Book of Death*. Oxford: Oxford University Press, 1983.

Epicurus. *Epicurus: The Extant Remains*, trans. Cyril Bailey. Oxford: Clarendon Press, 1926.

Ewing, A. C. *Non-Linguistic Philosophy*. London: George Allen & Unwin, 1968.

Feinberg, Joel. *Harm to Others*. New York: Oxford University Press, 1984.

Feinberg, Joel. *Rights, Justice and the Bounds of Liberty*. Princeton: Princeton University Press, 1980.

Flew, Antony. "Immortality." In *The Encyclopedia of Philosophy*, Vol. 4, pp. 139-150. Edited by Paul Edwards. New York: Macmillan, 1967.

Flew, Antony. *The Presumption of Atheism*. London: Elek/Pemberton, 1976.

Flew, Antony. "Tolstoi and the Meaning of Life." *Ethics* **73** (1963): 110-118.

Flew, R. Newton. *The Idea of Perfection in Christian Theology*. London: Oxford University Press, 1934.

Forrest, Peter. "Reincarnation Without Survival of Memory or Character." *Philosophy East and West* **28**(1978): 91-97.

Freud, Sigmund. "Thoughts for the Times on War and Death." In *The Standard Edition of the Complete Psychological Works of Sigmund Freud*, Vol. 14, pp. 272-302. London: Hogarth Press, 1957.

Frey, R. G. *Interests and Rights: The Case Against Animals*. Oxford: Clarendon Press, 1980.

Gandhi, Ramchandra. *The Availability of Religious Ideas*. London: Macmillan, 1976.

Geach, Peter. *God and the Soul*. London: Routledge & Kegan Paul, 1969.

Glasenapp, Helmuth von. *Immortality and Salvation in Indian Religions*, trans. E. F. J. Payne. Calcutta: Susil Gupta, 1963.

Glover, Jonathan. *Causing Death and Saving Lives*. Harmondsworth: Penguin, 1977.

Gombay, André. "What You Don't Know Doesn't Hurt You." *Proceedings of the Aristotelian Society* **79** (1978-79): 239-249.

Goodman, Nelson. *Of Mind and Other Matters*. Cambridge, Mass.: Harvard University Press, 1984.

Goodman, Nelson. *Problems and Projects*. Indianapolis: Bobbs-Merrill, 1972.

Goodman, Nelson. *Ways of Worldmaking*. Brighton: Harvester Press, 1978.

Green, Michael B. and Wikler, Daniel. "Brain Death and Personal Identity." *Philosophy and Public Affairs* **9** (1980): 105-133.

Green, O. H. "Fear of Death." *Philosophy and Phenomenological Research* **43** (1982): 99-105.

Haksar, Vinit. "Nagel on Subjective and Objective." *Inquiry* **24** (1981): 105-121.

Hare, R. M. *The Language of Morals*. Oxford: Clarendon Press, 1952.

Harrison, Jonathan. "Mackie's Moral 'Scepticism'." *Philosophy* **57** (1982): 173-191.

Harvie, J. A. "The Immortality of the Soul." *Religious Studies* **5** (1969): 207-222.

Head, Joseph and Cranston, S. L. eds. *Reincarnation in World Thought*. New York: Julian Press, 1967.

Heidegger, Martin. *Being and Time*, trans. John Macquarrie and Edward Robinson. London: SCM Press, 1962.

Hepburn, R. W. "Questions About the Meaning of Life." In *The Meaning of Life*, pp. 209-226. Edited by E. D. Klemke. New York: Oxford University Press, 1981.

Herbert, R. T. *Paradox and Identity in Theology*. Ithaca: Cornell University Press, 1979.

Herman, Arthur, L. *The Problem of Evil and Indian Thought*. Delhi: Motilal Banarsidass, 1976.

Heyd, David. "Is Life Worth Reliving?" *Mind* **92** (1983): 21-37.

Hick, John. *Arguments for the Existence of God*. London: Macmillan, 1970.

Hick, John. *Death and Eternal Life*. London: Collins, 1976.

Hick, John. *Evil and the God of Love*. London: Fontana, 1968.

Hick, John. *Faith and Knowledge*. 2nd ed. London: Macmillan, 1967.

Hick, John. *Philosophy of Religion*. 3rd ed. Englewood Cliffs, N. J.: Prentice-Hall, 1983.

Hick, John. "Theology and Verification." In *The Philosophy of Religion*, pp. 53-71. Edited by Basil Mitchell. London: Oxford University Press, 1971.

Hiriyanna, M. *Indian Conception of Values*. Mysore: Kavyalaya Publishers, 1975.

Hume, David. *Dialogues Concerning Natural Religion*, ed. Norman Kemp Smith. Indianapolis: Bobbs-Merrill, 1962.

Hume, David. "On the Immortality of the Soul." In *Hume on Religion*, pp. 263-270. Edited by Richard Wollheim. London: Fontana, 1963.

Hunter, J. F. M. *Essays After Wittgenstein*. Toronto: University of Toronto, 1973.

Johnstone, Henry, W., Jr. "Sleep and Death." *The Monist* **59** (1976): 218-233.

Kafka, Franz. *The Complete Stories*, ed. Nahum N. Glatzer. New York: Schocken Books, 1971.

Kant, Immanuel. *Critique of Practical Reason*, trans. Lewis White Beck. Indianapolis: Bobbs-Merrill, 1956.

Kass, Leon R. "Death as an Event: A Commentary on Robert Morison." In *Ethical Issues in Death and Dying*, pp. 70-81. Edited by Robert F. Weir. New York: Columbia University Press, 1977.

Kaufman, Arnold S. "Ability." *Journal of Philosophy* **60** (1963): 537-551.

Kesarcodi-Watson, Ian. "Can I Die?—An Essay in Religious Philosophy." *Religious Studies* **16** (1980): 163-178.

Klemke, E. D. ed. *The Meaning of Life*. New York: Oxford University Press, 1981.

Ladd, John. ed. *Ethical Issues Relating to Life and Death*. New York: Oxford University Press, 1979.

Lamb, David. "Diagnosing Death." *Philosophy and Public Affairs* **7** (1978): 144-153.

Langtry, Bruce. "In Defence of a Resurrection Doctrine." *Sophia* **21**(2) (1982): 1-9.

Larson, Gerald J. *Classical Sāmkhya*. 2nd rev. ed. Delhi: Motilal Banarsidass, 1979.

Leibniz, Gottfried Wilhelm. *Leibniz Selections*, ed. Philip P. Weiner. New York: Charles Scribner's Sons, 1951.

Levenbook, Barbara Baum. "Harming Someone after His Death." *Ethics* **94** (1984): 407-419.

Levenbook, Barbara Baum. "Harming the Dead, Once Again." *Ethics* **96** (1985): 162-164.

Lewis, Bernard. *The Assassins*. London: Weidenfeld and Nicolson, 1967.

Lewis, Hywel D. *The Elusive Self*. London: Macmillan, 1982.

Lewis, Hywel D. *Persons and Life After Death*. London: Macmillan, 1978.

Lewis, Hywel D. *The Self and Immortality*. London: Macmillan, 1973.

Lipner, J. J. "Hick's Resurrection." *Sophia* **18**(3) (1979): 22-34.

Locke, John. *An Essay Concerning Human Understanding*. Vol. 1, ed. A. C. Fraser. New York: Dover, 1959.

Lucretius. *De Rerum Natura*, trans. W. H. D. Rouse & M. F. Smith. Cambridge, Mass.: Harvard University Press, 1975.

MacGregor, Geddes. *Reincarnation as a Christian Hope*. London: Macmillan,1982.

Mackie, J. L. *The Cement of the Universe: A Study of Causation*. Oxford: Clarendon Press, 1974.

Mackie, J. L. *Ethics: Inventing Right and Wrong*. Harmondsworth: Penguin, 1977.

Mackie, J. L. "A Refutation of Morals." *Australasian Journal of Philosophy and Psychology* **24** (1946): 77-90.

Mackie, J. L. "Self-Refutation—A Formal Analysis." *Philosophical Quarterly* **14** (1964): 193-203.

McTaggart, J. M. E. *The Nature of Existence*. Vol. 2. Cambridge: Cambridge University Press, 1927.

McTaggart, J. M. E. *Some Dogmas of Religion*. London: Edward Arnold, 1906.

Madell, Geoffrey. *The Identity of the Self*. Edinburgh: Edinburgh University Press, 1981.

Mahābhārata. *The Mahabharata of Krishna-Dwaipayana Vyasa*. 4th ed. Vol. 9, trans. Kisari Mohan Ganguli. New Delhi: Munshiram Manoharlal, 1982.

Maṇḍana Miśra. *Brahmasiddhi by Ācārya Maṇḍanamiśra with commentary by Śaṅkhāpani*, ed. S. Kuppuswami Sastri. Madras: Government Oriental Manuscripts Library, 1937.

Mant, A. Keith. "The Medical Definition of Death." In *Man's Concern With Death*, pp. 13-24. By Arnold Toynbee *et al*. London: Hodder & Stoughton, 1968.

Margolis, Joseph. *Negativities: The Limits of Life*. Columbus, Ohio: Charles E. Merrill, 1975.

Marquis, Don. "Harming the Dead." *Ethics* **96** (1985): 159-161.

Matilal, Bimal Krishna. *Logical and Ethical Issues of Religious Belief*. Calcutta: University of Calcutta, 1982.

Moore, G. E. *Principia Ethica*. Cambridge: Cambridge University Press, 1903.

Morison, Robert S. "Death: Process or Event?" In *Ethical Issues in Death and Dying*, pp. 57-69. Edited by Robert F. Weir. New York: Columbia University Press, 1977.

Mothersill, Mary. "Death." In *Moral Problems*, pp. 372-383. Edited by James Rachels. New York: Harper & Row, 1971.

Murphy, Jeffrie G. "Rationality and the Fear of Death." *The Monist* **59** (1976): 187-203.

Nagel, Thomas. "The Limits of Objectivity." In *The Tanner Lectures On Human Values*, Vol. 1, pp. 77-139. Edited by Sterling M. McMurrin. Salt Lake City: University of Utah Press, 1980.

Nagel, Thomas. *Mortal Questions*. Cambridge: Cambridge University Press, 1979.

Nickelsburg, George W. E., Jr. *Resurrection, Immortality, and Eternal Life in Intertestamental Judaism*. Cambridge, Mass.: Harvard University Press, 1972.

Nietzsche, Friedrich. *The Gay Science*, trans. Walter Kaufmann. New York: Random House, 1974.

Nozick, Robert. "On the Randian Argument." *The Personalist* **52** (1971): 282-304.

Nozick, Robert. *Philosophical Explanations*. Cambridge Mass.: Harvard University Press, 1981.

Obeyesekere, Gananath. "Theodicy, Sin and Salvation in a Sociology of Buddhism." In *Dialectic in Practical Religion*, pp. 7-40. Edited by E. R. Leach. Cambridge: Cambridge University Press, 1968.

Oddie, Graham. "Control." In *Essays in Honour of Gwen Taylor*, pp. 190-221. Edited by R. G. Durrant. Dunedin: Philosophy Department, University of Otago, 1982.

Oddie, Graham. *Likeness to Truth*. Dordrecht: D. Reidel, 1986.

Oddie, Graham. "What Should We Do With Human Embryos?" *Interchange*, forthcoming.

O'Flaherty. Wendy Doniger, ed. *Karma and Rebirth in Classical Indian Traditions*. Berkeley: University of California Press, 1980.

O'Flaherty, Wendy Doniger. *The Origins of Evil in Hindu Mythology*. Berkeley: University of California Press, 1976.

Parfit, Derek. "Later Selves and Moral Principles." In *Philosophy and Personal Relations*, pp. 137-169. Edited by Alan Montefiore. Montreal: McGill-Queen's University Press, 1973.

Parfit, Derek. "On 'The Importance of Self-Identity'." *Journal of Philosophy* **68** (1971): 683-690.

Parfit, Derek. "Personal Identity." *Philosophical Review* **80** (1971): 3-27.

Parfit, Derek. *Reasons and Persons*. Oxford: Clarendon Press, 1984.

Partridge, Ernest. "Posthumous Interests and Posthumous Respect." *Ethics* **91** (1981): 243-264.

Pascal, Fania. "Wittgenstein: A Personal Memoir." In *Wittgenstein: Sources and Perspectives*, pp. 23-60. Edited by C. G. Luckhardt. Hassocks: Harvester Press, 1979.

Passmore, John. *The Perfectibility of Man*. New York: Charles Scribner's Sons, 1970.

Peirce, Charles Sanders. *Collected Papers*. Vol. 6. Edited by Charles Hartshorne & Paul Weiss. Cambridge, Mass.: Harvard University Press, 1935.

Penelhum, Terence. ed. *Immortality*. Belmont, California: Wadsworth, 1973.

Penelhum, Terence. *Survival and Disembodied Existence*. London: Routledge & Kegan Paul, 1970.

Penelhum, Terence. "Survival and Identity: Some Recent Discussions." In *Analytical Philosophy of Religion in Canada*, pp. 35-53. Edited by Mostafa Faghfoury. Ottawa: University of Ottawa, 1982.

Perrett, Roy W. "Dualistic and Nondualistic Problems of Immortality." *Philosophy East and West* **35** (1985): 333-350.

Perrett, Roy W. "Karma and the Problem of Suffering." *Sophia* **24**(1) (1985): 4-10.

Perrett, Roy W. "Rebirth." *Religious Studies*, forthcoming.

Perrett, Roy W. "Regarding Immortality." *Religious Studies*, forthcoming.

Perrett, Roy W. "Tolstoy, Death and the Meaning of Life." *Philosophy* **60** (1985): 231-245.

Perry, John. *A Dialogue on Personal Identity and Immortality* . Indianapolis: Hackett, 1978.

Phillips, D. Z. *Death and Immortality*. London: Macmillan, 1970.

Phillips, D. Z. and Dilman, İlham. *Sense and Delusion*. London: Routledge & Kegan Paul, 1971.

Pike, Nelson. *God and Timelessness*. London: Routledge & Kegan Paul, 1970.

Pitcher, George. "The Misfortunes of the Dead." *American Philosophical Quarterly* **21** (1984): 183-188.

Plato. *The Republic of Plato*, trans. F. M. Cornford. London: Oxford University Press, 1941.

Plotinus. *The Enneads*, trans. Stephen MacKenna. 2nd rev. ed. London: Faber & Faber, 1957.

Polo, Marco. *The Travels of Marco Polo*, trans. Ronald Latham. Harmondsworth: Penguin, 1958.

Poteat, William H. "Birth, Suicide and the Doctrine of Creation: An Exploration of Analogies." In *Religion and Understanding*, pp. 127-139. Edited by D. Z. Phillips. Oxford: Basil Blackwell, 1967.

Poteat, William H. "'I Will Die': An Analysis." In *Religion and Understanding*, pp. 199-213. Edited by D. Z. Phillips. Oxford: Basil Blackwell, 1967.

Potter, Karl H. ed. *Advaita Vedānta up to Śaṃkara and His Pupils*. Princeton: Princeton University Press, 1981.

Potter, Karl H. "Does Indian Epistemology Concern Justified True Belief?" *Journal of Indian Philosophy* **12** (1984): 307-327.

Potter, Karl H. "Freedom and Determinism from an Indian Perspective." *Philosophy East and West* **17** (1967): 113-124.

Potter, Karl H. ed. *Indian Metaphysics and Epistemology: The Tradition of Nyāya-Vaiśeṣika up to Gaṅgeśa*. Princeton: Princeton University Press, 1977.

Potter, Karl H. "Pre-existence." In *East-West Studies on the Problem of the Self*, pp. 193-207. Edited by P. T. Raju and Alburey Castell. The Hague: Martinus Nijhoff, 1968.

Potter, Karl H. *Presuppositions of India's Philosophies*. Englewood Cliffs, N. J.: Prentice-Hall, 1963.

Price, H. H. *Essays in the Philosophy of Religion*. Oxford: Clarendon Press, 1972.

Price, H. H. "Survival and the Idea of 'Another World'." In *Immortality*, pp. 21-47. Edited by Terence Penelhum. Belmont, Calif.: Wadsworth, 1973.

Priest, Graham. "Inconsistencies in Motion." *American Philosophical Quarterly* **22** (1985): 339-346.

Prior, Arthur N. *Papers in Logic and Ethics*. London: Duckworth, 1976.

Prior, Arthur N. *Papers on Time and Tense*. Oxford: Clarendon Press, 1968.

Puccetti, Roland. "The Conquest of Death." *The Monist* **59** (1976): 249-263.

Quinton, Anthony. "Spaces and Times." *Philosophy* **37** (1962): 130-147.

Radhakrishnan, Sarvepalli and Moore, Charles A. eds. *A Sourcebook in Indian Philosophy*. Princeton: Princeton University Press, 1957.

Rāmānuja. *The Vedānta-Sūtras With the Commentary by Rāmānuja*, trans. George Thibaut. Delhi: Motilal Banarsidass, 1962.

Rorty, Amélie Oksensberg. "Fearing Death." *Philosophy* **58** (1983): 175-188.

Rorty, Richard. *Consequences of Pragmatism (Essays: 1972-1980)*. Brighton: Harvester Press, 1982.

Rosenberg, Jay F. *Thinking Clearly About Death*. Englewood Cliffs, N. J.: Prentice-Hall, 1983.

Ryle, Gilbert. *The Concept of Mind*. Harmondsworth: Penguin, 1963.

Śaṃkara. *The Bṛhadāraṇyaka Upaniṣad with the Commentary of Śaṅkarācārya*. 4th ed., trans. Swāmī Mādhavānanda. Calcutta: Advaita Ashrama, 1965.

Śāntarakṣita. *The Tattvasaṅgraha of Śāntarakṣita with the Commentary of Kamalaśīla* . Vol. 2, trans. Ganganatha Jha. Baroda: Oriental Institute, 1939.

Schopenhauer, Arthur. *The World as Will and Representation* . Vol. 2, trans. E. F. J. Payne. New York: Dover, 1958.

Sherry, Patrick. *Religion, Truth and Language Games*. London: Macmillan, 1977.

Shibles, Warren. *Death: An Interdisciplinary Analysis*. Whitewater, Wisconsin: The Language Press, 1974.

Sidgwick, Henry. *The Methods of Ethics*. 7th ed. New York: Dover, 1966.

Silverstein, Harry S. "The Evil of Death." *Journal of Philosophy* **77** (1980): 401-424.

Skegg, P. D. G. *Law, Ethics, and Medicine*. Oxford: Clarendon Press, 1984.

Smart, Ninian. *Doctrine and Argument in Indian Philosophy*. London: George Allen & Unwin, 1964.

Smart, Ninian. *Philosophers and Religious Truth*. 2nd ed. London: SCM Press, 1969.

Smart, Ninian. "Philosophical Concepts of Death." In *Man's Concern with Death*, pp. 25-35. By Arnold Toynbee *et al.* London: Hodder & Stoughton, 1968.

Smart, Ninian. *Reasons and Faiths: An Investigation of Religious Discourse, Christian and Non-Christian*. London: Routledge & Kegan Paul, 1958.

Smart, Ninian. "Reincarnation." In *The Encyclopedia of Philosophy* , Vol. 7, pp. 122-124. Edited by Paul Edwards. New York: Macmillan, 1967.

Spence, Gordon William. *Tolstoy the Ascetic*. Edinburgh: Oliver & Boyd, 1967.

Spinoza, Benedict de. *Ethic*. 4th ed., trans. W. Hale White & Amelia H. Stirling. London: Oxford University Press, 1930.

Stcherbatsky, Th. *The Central Conception of Buddhism and the Meaning of the Word "Dharma"*. London: Royal Asiatic Society, 1923.

Stevenson, Ian. *Cases of the Reincarnation Type*. Vols. 1-3. Charlottesville: University of Virginia Press, 1975-79.

Stevenson, Ian. *The Evidence for Survival from Claimed Memories of Former Incarnations*. Tadworth: M. C. Peto, 1961.

Stevenson, Ian. *Twenty Cases Suggestive of Reincarnation*. 2nd rev. ed. Charlottesville: University of Virginia Press, 1974.

Strawson, P. F. "Social Morality and Individual Ideal." *Philosophy* **36** (1961): 1-17.

Sutherland, Stewart R. "Immortality and Resurrection." *Religious Studies* **3** (1968): 377-389.

Sutherland, Stewart R. "'What Happens After Death?'" *Scottish Journal of Theology* **22** (1969): 404-418.

Swift, Jonathan. *Gulliver's Travels*, ed. Herbert Davis. Oxford: Basil Blackwell, 1959.

Swinburne, R. G. "The Objectivity of Morality." *Philosophy* **51** (1976): 5-20.

Swinburne, R. G. "Personal Identity." *Proceedings of the Aristotelian Society* **74** (1973-74): 231-247.

Swinburne, R. G. "Persons and Personal Identity." In *Contemporary British Philosophy, Fourth Series*, pp. 221-237. Edited by H. D. Lewis. London: George Allen & Unwin, 1976.

Teilhard de Chardin, Pierre. *The Phenomenon of Man*. London: Collins, 1959.

Thomas Aquinas, Saint. *Summa Contra Gentiles*. Vol. 5, trans. English Dominican Fathers. London: Burns Oates & Washbourne, 1929.

Thomas Aquinas, Saint. *Summa Theologiae*. Vol. 2. London: Eyre & Spottiswoode, 1964.

Thornton, J. C. "Religious Belief and 'Reductionism'." *Sophia* **5** (3) (1966): 3-16.

Tichý, Pavel. "Kripke on Necessity A Posteriori." *Philosophical Studies* **43** (1983): 225-241.

Tola, Fernando and Dragonetti, Carmen. "*Anāditva* or Beginninglessness in Indian Philosophy." *Annals of the Bhandarkar Oriental Research Institute* **61** (1980): 1-20.

Tolstoy, Leo. *A Confession and The Gospel in Brief*. London: Oxford University Press, 1933.

Tolstoy, Leo. *Ivan Ilych and Hadji Murad*. London: Oxford University Press, 1934.

Tooley, Michael. *Abortion and Infanticide*. Oxford: Clarendon Press, 1983.

Tooley, Michael. "Decisions to Terminate Life and the Concept of Person." In *Ethical Issues Relating to Life and Death*, pp. 62-93. Edited by John Ladd. New York: Oxford University Press, 1979.

Toynbee, Arnold *et al. Man's Concern With Death*. London: Hodder & Stoughton, 1968.

Upaniṣads. *The Thirteen Principal Upanishads*. 2nd rev. ed., trans. Robert Ernest Hume. London: Oxford University Press, 1931.

Van Evra, James. "On Death as a Limit." *Analysis* **31** (1971): 170-176.

Walton, Douglas N. *On Defining Death: An Analytic Study of the Concept of Death in Philosophy and Medical Ethics*. Montreal: McGill-Queen's University Press, 1979.

Weber, Max. *The Religion of India*. New York: The Free Press, 1958.

Weber, Max. *The Sociology of Religion*. Boston: Beacon Press, 1963.

Weir, Robert F. ed. *Ethical Issues in Death and Dying*. New York: Columbia University Press, 1977.

Williams, Bernard. *Problems of the Self*. Cambridge: Cambridge University Press, 1973.

Wisdom, John. *Problems of Mind and Matter*. Cambridge: Cambridge University Press, 1934.

Wittgenstein, Ludwig. *Culture and Value*. ed. and trans. G. H. von Wright & Peter Winch. Oxford: Basil Blackwell, 1980.

Wittgenstein, Ludwig. *Philosophical Investigations*. 3rd ed., trans. G. E. M. Anscombe. Oxford: Basil Blackwell, 1968.

Wittgenstein, Ludwig. *Tractatus Logico-Philosophicus*, trans. D. F. Pears & B. F. McGuinness. London: Routledge & Kegan Paul, 1961.

Wolfson, Harry Austryn. *Religious Philosophy*. Cambridge, Mass.: Harvard University Press, 1961.

Wreen, Michael. "Mackie on the Objectivity of Values." *Dialectica* **39** (1985): 147-156.

Young, Robert. "The Resurrection of the Body." *Sophia* **9**(2) (1970): 1-15.

Zemach, Eddy M. "Love Thy Neighbour as Thyself or Egoism and Altruism." In *Studies in Ethical Theory*, pp. 148-158. Edited by Peter A. French *et al*. Morris: University of Minnesota, 1978.

INDEX